In Dreams

A Life Journey In Prose and Poetry

Elizabeth Grandbois

Manor House Publishing Inc.

National Library of Canada
Cataloguing in Publication Data:

Grandbois, Elizabeth, 1952-
In Dreams
A Life Journey In Prose and Poetry / Elizabeth Grandbois

ISBN 978-1-897453-88-9

    I.   Title.

PS8563.R352915 2002   C811'6   C2002-905156-8
PR9199.4.G7215 2002

Copyright 2002-10-15
By Elizabeth Grandbois/Manor House Publishing.
Published November 15, 2002
by Manor House Publishing Inc.
(905) 648-2193

First Edition.
Autobiography in 4 Parts. 128 pages. 67 poems.
All rights reserved.
Cover Design: Michael B. Davie.
Cover layout/realization: Richard Kosydar.

Acknowledgements

This book would not have been possible without the thoughtful support of a great many people, far too many to name.

However, I would like to mention just a few names and hope the others forgive their exclusion. All of you know who you are. And you know I deeply appreciate everything you've done for me.

I'd be remiss if I did not thank my husband Marc and our children Renee, Philippe and Andre for their solid support, compassion and understanding. I may be the one who is terminally ill with amyotrophic lateral sclerosis (ALS), but I am not coping with this alone. I am surrounded with the love of my family.

I'd also like to thank all those who have played a role in making the annual Elizabeth's Concert of Hope a success. Again, there are too many to list them all. But it's the support of these wonderful people that has helped these concerts raise funds to fight ALS – also known as Lou Gehrig's Disease.

Thanks also to Murray McLauchlan for taking time from his singer/songwriter/musician career to thoughtfully write the book's 'Foreword'.

As well, I'd like to thank Michael B. Davie for writing the 'Afterword', his project vision and editing work; and his Manor House Publishing company for allowing me to share my prose and poetry.

Finally, my thanks to ALS Canada for this organization's tremendous efforts in the fight against Lou Gehrig's Disease. If you'd like to support these efforts, please contact ALS Canada for more details. Phone: 1-800-267-4257. Website: www.als.ca.

- Elizabeth Grandbois.

Contents:

Acknowledgements
About The Author
Foreword
Afterword

My Story: Autobiography in 4 parts:
Accompanied by selections of poetry.

Part 1
My Story
17 poems

Part 2
Family, Friends and Fighting Back
15 poems

Part 3
Learning Life's Lesson
18 poems

Part 4
In Dreams
17 poems
Closing Thoughts

Manor House Publishing Inc.
(905) 648-2193.

About the author

With a true gift for engaging readers, Elizabeth Grandbois is one of the most interesting poets to emerge on the Canadian scene in years.

Grandbois is afflicted with amyotrophic lateral sclerosis, or ALS (Lou Gehrig's Disease), a progressive fatal neuromuscular disease that causes muscles to lose strength, eventually resulting in paralysis and death.

The terminally ill author has infused much of her writing with a sense of immediacy borne of trying to cope with a fatal disease for which there is no cure.

Indeed, Grandbois' poetry has an intensity owed to her own heightened sense of mortality.

Born and raised in Hamilton, Elizabeth Ann MacFarlane was second-youngest of five children.

After spending her childhood in Hamilton, she studied nursing in Toronto and met and married Marc Grandbois shortly after graduating in 1973.

However, her nursing career ended when she was diagnosed with ALS in 1998.

Grandbois immediately began fighting ALS, advocating and fund-raising, organizing benefit concerts, public speaking tours and media interviews.

She's been the subject of a seemingly endless stream of newspaper and magazine articles, radio and television programs.

Grandbois has been a guest on such popular programs as The Vicki Gabereau Show, Canada AM, CBC's Health Matters, Michael Coren Live, the Life Network and Discovery TV's Health program.

Radio show's have included CBC Radio's First Person Singular, where she read aloud her own story of ALS before a receptive, responsive national audience.

Grandbois is also the source of inspiration behind Elizabeth's Concert of Hope, the annual benefit concerts that raise funds for the ALS Society in the fight against Lou Gehrig's Disease. Concert performers have included Murray McLauchlan, Ian Thomas, the Nylons and many other legendary acts.

She's also raised awareness of ALS through her public speaking tours and lectures on behalf of ALS Canada: 1-800-267-425. Website: www.als.ca.

Grandbois is also raising ALS awareness through her captivating prose and poetry.

Not that all of her poems purely deal with her disease. Many poems carry messages of hope, insightful observations and deep insight into the art of living and the ability to love the gift of life.

Some of her critically acclaimed poetry was previously published by the Tower Poetry Society. Her poem The Lure of Sleep provided the theme for the National Symposium of Sleep Disorders at the University of Toronto. And her poem In Dreams was the highlight of ALS Fundraising Walk 2001 Closing Ceremonies.

Cherish Each Day, her own story of life with ALS, was featured in Canadian Living Magazine, reaching a responsive national audience.

In an unprecedented move, Canadian Living recently responded to an outpouring of concern from its readers by running an article assuring them that Elizabeth's ALS is now progressing more slowly and she's focusing on her writing.

Grandbois currently resides in Burlington with her husband Marc, and their children: Renee, Philippe and Andre.

In Dreams is her first book of poetry.

Foreword

By Murray McLauchlan

It was a bright afternoon in the fall of 2001 when I received a phone call from my friend, fellow musician Ian Thomas.

Ian was calling with a request: He said he was hosting an event called "Elizabeth's Concert of Hope" in the coming February. He named some of the other artists who had pitched in and asked me if I'd perform at this concert.

Then Ian told me about Elizabeth Grandbois, explaining that she was a friend of the family and a wonderful person.

He also explained that Elizabeth has been diagnosed with ALS – Lou Gehrig's Disease – and the purpose of the concert was to raise funds and awareness levels in the fight against this fatal and, so far, incurable disease.

I knew something about ALS.

When Ian called, it had only been a few months since my brother-in-law passed away from Lou Gehrig's Disease. It had been extremely distressing watching him become slowly imprisoned within his own body. It had been very hard on his family.

I told Ian that I would be happy to play the concert.

It was a gala evening with a packed and appreciative audience filling the DuMaurier Theatre in Hamilton, Ontario. It wasn't a solemn occasion at all. It was instead lively and full of fun.

At the end, as Elizabeth came on stage with her walker, there was a breaking wave of heartfelt, spontaneous applause that grew and grew as she stood and faced the audience. It was recognition of her courage, the force of her personality and her formidable determination to make a difference.

After the show, I was introduced to Elizabeth. But rather than thanks and goodbye, it turned out to be more of a beginning.

Elizabeth asked for permission to e-mail me and periodic correspondence began.

She came up to Ottawa and attended a show I performed at the National Arts Centre. She came to my home in Toronto with a member of the organizing group of the Concert of Hope with a view to exploring the possibility of expanding into other areas. I had a chance to talk with, and listen to, Elizabeth.

Maybe it's the urgency that underlies her terminal condition that drives her honesty, but I think her frankness and disarming candour are simply inherent in her personality. She showed a willingness to reveal joys, doubts, fears and cut to the chase that I found refreshing and disarming.

Elizabeth is not an illness. She is a person coping with an illness. She has a tremendous intelligence and a lot of love in her, love that has caused her to take what has happened to her and see that there may be some way to draw good from the experience and help others, if she can.

Cynical people might dismiss all of this as a coping mechanism. It would be a better world if there was less cynicism. I found myself responding to the love in Elizabeth by loving her right back – myself and a lot of other people.

This may sound odd, but after our first meeting, I never gave another thought to her condition. I simply accepted her as she was at that moment.

I remember marvelling once, after the death of my mother, that I had never thought of my mother as being old, even though I knew she was in her seventies.

It had to do with the spirit in her eyes.

Elizabeth has that kind of spirit shining in her eyes and it tends to blind me to the grim reality that she really won't be around all that long, barring a miracle. It also gives me the licence to be able to kid her some.

It makes more poignant her revelation that she now hides her smile behind her hand because she isn't sure what her facial muscles are actually doing. Her smile is beautiful!

But this is a Foreword to a book that is part autobiography, part poetry.

I think Elizabeth asks that we accept her, not as a writer with ALS, but simply as a writer, chronicling her experiences. There is much here that has to do with other matters.

Elizabeth is taking us on a journey and allowing us into her life in a most intimate way, from her first halting efforts at poetry as a form of therapy, writing out of desperation and fear in the wee small hours, to her evolution over time into a full fledged poet who writes to elevate herself above her condition and succeeds and carrying others along with her.

Everywhere in this book there are gems: 'The Goalie' is a wonderful reminisce on minor hockey and parental love. 'Little Lamb' breaks your heart with its story of holding a dying infant in the wee small hours of a hospital night. 'Illness' gives full reign to anger and acceptance in the same work. 'Clothesline News' is a funny, offbeat take on hanging laundry.

Slowly but surely, as the book progresses, we see the unfolding wonder of Elizabeth finding her voice. It is a strong voice, full of life and compassion.

If I have one regret, it is that she did not begin this work much earlier in her life. She is on a journey and I pray that God will give her the time and strength to go as far as she wants.

- Murray McLauchlan,
singer/songwriter/musician,
Toronto, Canada, 2002.

Afterword

By Michael B. Davie

Elizabeth Grandbois immediately captured my attention the moment I first saw this attractive and intriguing lady.

She seemed to have an other-worldly aura about her, an air of serenity that invited anyone in her presence to return her welcoming smile.

And she was in a wheelchair – rolling her way toward me from the other end of a living room.

It was early December 2001. We were both among invited guests attending the Tower Poetry Society's Annual Christmas Party.

My dual role of writer and publisher had won me a spot on the guest list and I joined those turning up at the Dundas home of a fellow poet.

I had also published a book of poems – Mystical Poetry by Deborah Morrison – and had taken this Hamilton poet with me to the party.

We were barely through the front door when Deborah was happily chatting with those inside, letting everyone who'd listen know how pleased she was that I'd published her first book of poetry.

I was suddenly showered with attention – I was the only publisher in a house full of poets.

My assurances, that I'd consider the poetic works of those present but could make no promises, spread rapidly, person-to-person, through the room.

By the time the buzz reached Elizabeth, the message had changed: Now I was apparently willing to publish everyone's work. Sight unseen.

Moments later, Elizabeth pulled up beside me and in a weak, wavering voice told me how happy she was to learn of my interest in publishing the works of those present, as she had a children's book to publish.

Elizabeth confided that she was terminally ill with ALS – Lou Gehrig's Disease – and she had approached few publishers with her poetry for fear of what impact the stress might have on her very frail condition should her poems be rejected.

It was an awkward situation. But I needn't have worried: Elizabeth recited her Scarecrow poem from memory – I was hooked. Her poem touched me with its message of isolation and loneliness, beauty and despair. And I wanted to read more.

Elizabeth shyly, cheerfully obliged, offering me a collection of truly outstanding poetry: 'Buried', 'Shoe Lessons', 'The Visitor', 'When You're Grown', 'Clothesline News' (the pants are, my friend, a-blowin' in the wind), 'Illness', and many more great poems.

Elizabeth's poems skilfully paint pictures in your mind, confront your emotions, invade your thoughts, touch your soul.

I soon realized our meeting had been fateful. And I envisioned more than a children's book: It would be a legacy book containing her life story and poetry.

Thank you Elizabeth for sharing your deep and profound appreciation of life and loved ones.

It is a privilege to publish your first book of prose and poetry, a legacy book that will live on, long after you're taken from us too soon.

Thanks to your poetry, we'll always share your love for Summer Rain. We'll look for you by The Willow Tree. And we'll find you… In Dreams.

- **Michael B. Davie,** publisher, author, Winning Ways.

My Story
Part One

Knowledge of my destiny has distanced me from the rest of the world but at the same time has given me a new appreciation of life and a deeper understanding of the value of the time I've been given.

I've come to believe that it's not so much what we do or say as how we have made others feel that will have the greatest impact in the end.

This is my story, a story that started out like a fairy tale and suddenly changed into a nightmare.

It now reads like a dream difficult to interpret and ever changing.

My name is Elizabeth Ann and I am 48 years old. I have been a nurse for 27 years and a mother for 22 years. Right up until the late 1990s, my life was remarkably uncomplicated.

A happy childhood

I grew up in Hamilton, Ontario the fourth daughter of five children.

I had three older sisters, Jennifer, Maureen, Kathryn and one younger brother, Jamie.

I think I was supposed to be the boy, but it didn't turn out that way.

Family dynamics had us divided into two groups, the three girls and my brother and I.

It worked well this way: The three older girls were kept very busy with their music activities, an undercurrent of competition keeping them focused, while Jamie and I were left to our own resources.

We amused ourselves well in those early years spending hours playing imaginary games and just quietly keeping each other company.

There was only 2 ½ years age difference between us and we were best of friends.

Escape to a secret place

I remember so well our little outings early in the morning before anyone was awake.

I would have been about five years old. Lady, our dog, a pretty Border Collie, always knew when we were going out.

She would sit patiently, tail brushing softly on the floor while we pulled our coats over our flannel pajamas.

Once the back door was open she would bound ahead turning circles impatient for us to get going.

The wagonload of stuffed animals was still there at the side of the house, untouched since our last adventure.

One of us would pull the wagon, with the other following across the road to the path that led into the woods.

There were beautiful soft grasses growing at the foot of the trees and in one little area not far from the path there was a large patch of soft, fairy grass that we called "Greenland".

It was our own secret place we shared with neighborhood friends.

Sometimes we would bring snacks and drinks and spend the afternoon lying on the grass telling stories.

Our morning outings didn't last long.

Feeling the pangs of hunger, we would turn our little "Wellington boots" in the direction of home where we would settle in front of the black and white television to watch 'The Three Stooges'.

Alpha bits was our staple at 6 am, so while Jamie kept track of the antics of Curly Larry and Mo, I would quietly sneak into the kitchen, careful to avoid the creaky spots in the floor and climb on the counter to reach this box of sugary treats.

Under the chestnut tree

I remember fall days when we played under the chestnut tree collecting the prickly green fruit.

We would sit beside each other and with great care peel the skin back to reveal the smooth, moist brown chestnuts – 'conkers' as we used to call them.

My parents had a happy marriage and we lived comfortably in a big ranch style house at the edge of the escarpment (Hamilton Mountain).

My father was a doctor, a tall, soft spoken man who rose early each day to eat his bowl of porridge and be away to the hospital by 7 a.m.

He never left the house without giving Mom a hug and a kiss good bye.

At the end of the day, usually after we had finished dinner, Dad would return home to quickly and quietly eat his own meal, which had been kept warm over a simmering pot of water and then leave again for an evening meeting.

My mother was very protective of my father, discouraging noisy play or sibling rivalry when he was around.

We were constantly reminded of the importance of Dad's work. We were not allowed to talk to friends on the phone in case the hospital was trying to reach him.

To me he seemed gentle with a reserved, even temper, sometimes untouchable, someone you would never want to disappoint.

Quiet dad, busy mom

Mom was always busy. She stayed at home organizing the household and her brood.

She was quick to loudly voice her disapproval of behavior or performance.

But she was always there to support her children's activities and protect their well being.

Mom loved music and she loved to sing.

She glowed when we were decked out in choir gowns standing shoulder to shoulder.

I remember one Easter Sunday before church feeling silly that we were all in gray flannel coats with black paten shoes and new Easter bonnets.

Even my brother matched with his flannel shorts and knee socks, hair combed as slick as could be with the cowlick refusing to cooperate.

Being a group of five children, there was no opportunity for individuality – we conformed in the early years knowing we had no choice.

Mom spent her days planning menus, washing clothes, organizing her cleaning help and driving us to our extra curricular activities, primarily music lessons and choir practices.

Because I grew up in such a controlled, secure environment I was free to be a child, to play childish games and indulge in childish imaginings.

I didn't really spend much time with my parents, Mom was too busy and Dad was always gone.

I felt more connected to my siblings.

Unfortunately they never wanted to include me in their activities.

I was too young and by the time my brother was seven he had a best friend, Scott.

This left me mostly on my own from the age of seven. I quite enjoyed playing by myself.

I was happy with my own thoughts and fantasies.

Life on the edge

I loved our big house. It was situated on the edge of the Niagara escarpment overlooking the downtown of the city of Hamilton.

I remember getting up at night in the dark to stand at my window looking down at the magic city lights. It was like a jewel box.

During the day, I would sometimes look out the window to the rooftops below and wonder what the people were doing in each of those houses at that very moment. I could stand there for long periods just imagining.

Our house was a wonderful setting for 'hide and seek'.

Hiding places seemed endless; closets, cupboards and attic rooms.

My favorite hiding spot was a little cupboard beside the kitchen table where we stored the TV tables.

Now that I think of it, one had to be quite small to fit in there.

Upstairs, there were two secret attic doors, one inside one of the big hall closets and the other inside my brother's bedroom closet.

These attic rooms led to small, dark, scary spaces beneath the roof.

In the attic in the hall there was an old blue metal trunk where the Halloween costumes and dress-up clothes were stored for special occasions.

Monsters in the attic

I would open the little attic door just wide enough to reach my arm up and in, pulling hard on the chain hanging from the light bulb.

I pulled it quickly – imaginary monsters were always a threat.

When the small room was lit I would bravely go over to the trunk and take out the beautiful black wig with two long braids.

It was part of an Indian princess costume, one I wasn't supposed to touch except at Halloween.

For a little girl with short brown hair, it made me feel beautiful, and if no one was home I would come out in the hall and dance in front of the full length mirror, the braids swinging with my movements. The fantasy was so real for that short time alone.

When Mom went out I occasionally got up the courage to invite neighborhood friends over.

We would hide and seek until she came back and shooed us all outside to play. I hated being outside – I always preferred to be in my room playing imaginary games.

Summers were spent at our cottage in Muskoka, where there was always something to occupy our time.

We spent hours under the hot summer sun, sun tanning and frequently comparing tan lines under our swimsuits.

When we had sufficiently baked ourselves we would delight in water-skiing or "gunnel-bobbing," a game we played with the canoe. This was a game for two, preferably strong swimmers, usually my sisters.

With the canoe in the water, each person would stand on the gunnels, or sides of the canoe, one at each end and rock the canoe up and down until one lost their balance. Usually when one fell off the other followed shortly thereafter.

Idyllic cottage life

There were so many cottage games that we played like 'kick the can' and 'poke in the back,' games my father taught us.

At night in the dark we would run down to the lake to 'skinny dip', wrapped in only beach towels. We would hide our towels behind the rocks fearing some unknown "voyeur" would steal them and leave us stranded.

The ink, black water was cold against our warm skin. It was exciting treading water beside each other, our squeals of excitement breaking the silence of the night air.

It was during the cottage days that I learned about monarch butterflies. I was ten years old.

I always looked forward to the weekend when my father would leave the city and come and join us at the cottage.

On this particular weekend I brought him a fat, yellow and black striped caterpillar that I had found on one of the poplar trees.

He told me to go and find three more and when I had them in my little plastic pot, we carefully placed them in the cardboard box that we filled with young poplar branches and leaves.

I taped saran wrap tightly to the hole I had cut in the side for a window.

Over the following weeks I watched these fat, colorful creatures make homes for themselves and emerge from their green pupas as beautiful orange and black butterflies. This is one of my favorite memories.

It was experiences like these that gave me a love of nature and respect for all living things.

I also loved playing in the woods at the cottage and spent many hours in a secret place down by the lake. As children, we really didn't know how lucky we were.

Lonely adolescence

During my early adolescence I found summer days at the cottage lonely and frustrating.

I had a boyfriend nearby but he seemed more interested in my older sister.

He was from a family of seven boys, all good looking and funny.

I was desperate to see him and would have gone down to his cottage every day except for my fear of the herd of unfriendly cows outside our property.

They had already chased us once and I wasn't going to test them again. I remember the one day I was so determined to see my boyfriend. I decided to swim to his cottage. It was half a mile down the shore.

I set out and when I got to the dock his brother, with a mildly amused tone told me he wasn't home.

I felt embarrassed and foolish at having to turn around and swim back.

Wonderful camp memories

My best memories were my summers at camp in Algonquin Park, from the age of twelve to sixteen. I felt so confident, we all wore tan and green uniforms and the equality of our dress allowed our personalities to emerge.

These were wonderful days full of new experiences. I took sailing and canoeing lessons; I practiced archery and learned how to high dive; I experienced the Northern lights and the melancholy cry of the loon; I encountered an angry bear and made friends with the chipmunks.

During our week long canoe trips I learned how to portage and make a fire even in the most inclement weather.

Sleeping under the stars in my sleeping bag huddled next to a smoking fire, telling ghost stories was so exciting. I was always sad to leave at the end of the two months. I think I felt a greater sense of self when I was away from home. I missed the family while I was at camp but being the youngest had its disadvantages.

When summer ended and winter holidays came around we'd climb into slippery ski suits and pile into the station wagon. Skis and poles were strapped tightly to the car's roof rack as we headed to ski slopes in Quebec… (to be continued in Part 2, after the following selection of poems)

Childhood is a wonderful time of life. Perhaps these poems will conjure up some memories of your own?

Poems of Childhood

Elizabeth Grandbois, September 1999: At the cottage I played for long periods in the woods. I remember well the secret place...

A Secret Place

When I was very young I had a secret place,
in amongst the birch trees
down beside the lake.
Fallen autumn leaves carpeted the ground,
there was a log to sit on
and a boulder, smooth and round.
Sitting very quietly, I'd wait for guests to come,
fairies, elves or wood folk,
I'd welcome anyone.
A black and yellow caterpillar crawling on a tree
left its signature of lace
on a young green leaf.
The lapping sound of water as it rolled along the shore
made it difficult to hear the little voices,
but when I heard them whispering
I felt such great delight,
for **they** *had come to play with me*
...albeit out of sight.

Elizabeth Grandbois, December 1999
Nature has always been a friend…

The Willow Tree

*My journey leads me down a road
beside a sheltered lee,
it forks along a narrow point
around a willow tree.
And there I stop to rest awhile
the branches weeping low,
the shade is cool, the ground is soft,
it's soothing to the soul.
I lean my back against the trunk,
the tree feels wise and strong,
I close my eyes and listen
to its tranquil rustling.
I tell the tree my story
where I come from, who I am,
I share my load of worries
with this tall and willowy friend.
I rise again to take the road
much lighter in my mind,
the tree will guard my secrets
I can leave them all behind.*

Elizabeth Grandbois, October 1999
One lovely memory is that of a dream I used to have regularly as a child. It was a wonderful dream.

My Flying Dream

*I sometimes close my eyes
and pretend that I can fly,
I used to have just such a dream.
The wind would lift my body
and make me feel so light,
a pleasure only known in dreams,
a freedom felt in flight.
I'd look down upon the people,
they seemed to be so small,
it's strange they never noticed
never noticed me at all.
Floating on the gentle breeze
I'd circle 'round and 'round
and when I grew too tired
my feet would touch the ground.
Sadly, it was just a dream
that brought me such delight,
I dearly hope my flying dream
will come to me tonight.*

Young Camper

Lying in my bunk bed feeling toasty warm,
I wondered what had wakened me
in the early light of dawn.
The bugle hadn't sounded for campers to arise,
the other girls were sleeping
I could hear their restful sighs.
Then I heard the rustling from underneath my bunk,
looking down beneath the cot,
I saw the small chipmunk.
He was right there in the corner sitting bold as brass,
nibbling on the cookies
I had hidden in my pack.
He'd tasted each and every one
and left a pile of crumbs,
I wouldn't have minded sharing, if he'd only eaten one.
Suddenly, the bugle broke the silence of the morn
and before the bugler finished,
the little thief was gone.
I was sorry when he ran away
and wished to see him back
so I planned to entice him
with a tempting little snack.
That night I placed a tid-bit underneath my bunk
and what I didn't want to share
I hid inside my trunk.
The little chipmunk did return along with other friends,
a host of furry visitors running under beds.
We watched this curious caper, taking all in jest,
...no one ever questioned,
    who'd invited all the guests.

The Resident Snake

He viewed his jurisdiction from atop the granite rock
coiled in perfect symmetry he basked beneath the sun
passers-by were monitored along the flagstone path,
some of them he shadowed and some he left alone.

The path was the link from the cottage to the shore,
the necessary passage for those who liked to bathe,
reckless toads and chipmunks
crossed the rough terrain,
rushing to the poplar grove, believing they were safe.

Now and then, the furtive snake
would up and disappear,
causing more alarm, when hiding out of sight,
but by and large he spent his day sunning on the stone,
storing all his energy for foraging at night.

As children we felt anxious
by this most unwelcome guest,
we tirelessly begged he be taken far away,
acquiescing to our pleas, father found a canvas bag
and paddled with his charge to the far end of the bay.

At last we were free from the shady silhouette,
with emancipated joy we skipped toward the lake,
it had only been a day since the dweller was evicted
yet here he was, back again,
the dreaded resident snake.

He viewed his jurisdiction from atop the granite rock,
coiled in perfect symmetry he basked beneath the sun,
passers-by were monitored along the flagstone path,
some of them he shadowed and some he left alone.

Elizabeth Grandbois, February 2000: I've always loved the fresh clean air just after it rains.

Summer Rain

Sitting on my veranda in the old wooden chair,
I knew a storm was brewing.
I felt anticipation as clouds moved overhead,
the hot humid morning weighed me down like lead.
There was deep, distant rumbling,
skies were growing dark,
with a loud clap of thunder the rain began to pour.
Worms were drawn to puddles
as rain came splashing down,
birds would soon be feasting
on their meal from underground.
The soggy looking daisies drooped their pretty heads,
as rivulets of water ran throughout the garden beds.
Then as the rain subsided, and skies began to clear,
I raised my head and took a breath
of cool refreshing air.
I've always loved the summer,
in that old wooden chair
sitting on my veranda when the rain begins to fall.

Elizabeth Grandbois, February 2000:
This was written for the love and wonder of nature;
beautiful yet sometimes cruel.

The Hawk

He sat high upon the wire
surveying harrowed field,
his beady eyes focused
on another savoury meal.
With beak tucked low,
he cocked his head,
targeting his find
planning when to make his move.
Preparing for the long descent,
he slowly stretched his wings,
perched with poise and purpose.
Suddenly he swooped down low,
talons to the ground,
and snatched the unsuspecting prize,
caught without a sound.
Soaring high towards the east
he swung his tender prey,
and headed for the soft brown nest.
He landed there upon the branch,
and offered up the food,
to mother hawk, the guardian,
protector of the brood.
Then off again and soaring,
gliding high up in the sky,
he waited for another mouse
to catch his beady eye.

Elizabeth Grandbois, March 2000:
As a child, clowns always frightened me.

Image of A Clown

*Look closely at this man masquerading as a clown,
his skin is painted white, a teardrop on his cheek,
the ruby red smile that's drawn from ear to ear,
is curiously bigger than a smile's supposed to be.*

*His stares into the crowd, never once a blink,
the whites of his eyes have a sickly yellow hue,
the bulbous rubber nose, a deep fuchsia pink,
clashes with cheeks deftly smudged with rouge.*

*The floppy velvet hat that falls off his head,
reveals a tangled mop of hair, a gaudy olive green,
soft, satin ruffles at the neck, arms and feet,
contradict the soulful image of the man I see.*

*In farcical performance he plays the great buffoon,
grotesque in his movements, with huge brown shoes,
reflecting on his antics, he gives a humble shrug,
appealing to the audience, who applaud him as a fool.*

*I see the sorrow in his face, a smile that's never there
his look passes through me if I chance to meet his eye,
the face paint and the costume change the man into a*
                                                                clown,
he may think I've been fooled, but the spirit never lies.

Elizabeth Grandbois, March 2000:
The endless adventure that is nature…

Night's Charm

*I slipped out very quietly in the darkness of the night,
visiting my roses, their fragrance sweetly light.*

*Fireflies danced elusively lighting up the sky,
such tiny wondrous sparkles, dazzling to the eye.*

*Mist was swirling at my feet blanketing the ground,
I tiptoed on the pathway, making ne'er a sound.*

*Lonely little crickets chirped beneath the garden gate,
hiding in the long wet grass calling for their mate.*

*I leaned against the weathered fence
to wish upon a star,
in hopes the twinkling asterisk
could hear me from afar.*

*The harmony of nature as I stood there on my own,
gave credence to an inner sense that I was not alone.*

Elizabeth Grandbois, March 2000: I love Algonquin Park, the Northern lights, the call of the Loon…

Spirit Of The North

Feel the essence of creation in the forests of the north,
stand among the firs that yield to gentle winds,
breathe the scent of pine that pervades the northern air,
step amidst the scattered fruit these mighty trees have given.

Take time to watch the sun as it slips into the lake,
catch the last glimpse of pink as veil of night descends,
see the water change from blue to darkest ink,
bathe in the moonlight where the shoreline meets the land.

Nocturnal sounds surround you as you settle down to sleep,
listen to the hoot owl searching out her prey,
the elusive loon will haunt you with a melancholy wail,
crying to her soul mate as she swims along the bay.

Huddle close together near the heat of evening's fire,
draw sleeping bags closer to the red embers' glow,
romanced by nature's beauty, fall into dreamless sleep,
resting 'til the dawn returns and campfires have grown cold.

Elizabeth Grandbois, April 2000: I was lucky as a child to have the privilege of cottage life.

Summertime

Come sit with me we'll reminisce
of times we used to know,
when youth was blessed by innocence.
Memories of endless days beneath a radiant sun,
swimming in a crystal lake
'til daylight hours were done.
Simple card games won and lost on rainy afternoons,
listening to the "hit parade."
We'll laugh about the "skinny dipping"
 under moonlit skies,
hiding towels behind the rocks,
away from peering eyes
Buttered popcorn, "kick the can,"
playing "hide and seek,"
secrets in the "bunky" forgotten in our sleep.
These will be our keepsakes when all is said and done,
days of childhood pleasures,
kissed by summer's sun.

Elizabeth Grandbois, February 2000: We used to sail in the summertime. I long to return to those endless, carefree days of summer.

Young Sailors

It was a perfect day for sailing, we stepped into the boat,
patterns on the lake showed a gently blowing wind,
we hoisted up the sails as they flapped their discontent,
preparing for the pull and tug that soon was to begin.

Freeing up the bow and stern, we pulled the main sail tight,
our vessel started moving leaving moorings far behind,
Sails fluffed gently in the wind, a soft rippling sound,
the boat cut through waters, that lapped along its side.

Further out upon the lake we tightened up the jib,
catching the prevailing winds that filled the canvas sails,
the starboard side plunged to meet the fast flowing wash,
behind the boat, the wake left its long dark tail.

Feet pressed to the centre, we sat high upon the side,
our heads out over water as we leaned against the pull,
with wet hair in the wind, we yelled in sheer delight,
feeling the vibrations of the rudder as she heeled.

Then suddenly our ship lost wind and sails began to flap,
we pulled the tiller to the left and brought the boat about,
the boom swung low to port side, clanging on the mast,
pressing on with billowed sails, we tacked toward the south.

We spent the day out on the lake, sailing wild and free,
challenging Mother Nature and the forces of her will,
letting go of the timewewere lost to sailors dreams,
returning home at sundown with the early evening chill.

Elizabeth Grandbois, August 2001:
Some of my best friends have feathers…

Feathered Friends

*Dainty little goldfinch
delicately picking seed,
indifferent to your feathered friends
who peck and fight to feed.*

*Why can't you teach them manners,
how to wait a turn,
are they so uncouth
or too ill-bred to learn?*

*Call them to attention
from your perch up in the tree,
show them how to choose a seed
and crack it tenderly.*

*For if they are more gracious ,
less will go to waste
and I will then be more inclined
to feed them everyday.*

Return voyage

Sail me away on the crest of a wave
gentle winds nudging behind,
reflections of moonlight guiding the way,
carry me weightless in time.

Soothed by the movement of tides
I'm rocked in the ebb and the flow,
returned to the soul of the universe,
there where my spirit was born.

Long Way Home

The way is tortuous,
unfamiliar,
a daunting journey
born without warning
If I lead with my heart
my soul will follow,
and the path I find
might one day
bring me home.

Elizabeth Grandbois. April 2002:
Who knew going nowhere could be such fun?

Call of the Carousel

*Sweet sounds of the carousel
carry me back in time,
circling round and round
to a moment of musical enchantment,
where gilt, painted ponies gently rise
on their polished silver poles,
and undulating movements begin,
up and own.
What magic we create in the circular game,
a simple tinkling of melodies,
to captivate and delight,
as this pretty baroque herd
turns past old chestnut trees and lamp posts,
round and round,
up and down,
whirling us far from weariness,
and the familiar faces,
and places
of everyday life.*

Elizabeth Grandbois, January 2000:
This is the last straw...

The Scarecrow

There's a scruffy old scarecrow standing in the corn,
his checkered shirt is tattered, his leather hat is worn.
His weather beaten trousers are flapping in the wind,
and those hands and feet of straw
are looking mighty thin.

He's posted like a sentinel guarding crops of maize,
all trespassers are subject to his stony watchful gaze.
The blackbirds seem to know him
as if he were a friend
assuming that his job was to be
guarding corn for them.

They perch along his outstretched arms
and sit upon his hat,
pecking at each other and cawing at the cat.
Cat keeps scarecrow company, he's never very far,
all curled up at scarecrow's feet, sleeping on the straw.

The children come to visit, playing hide and seek,
feasting on the yellow corn, picked so young and sweet
They love this sun-kissed ragman
standing tall and proud,
the colourful custodian of their field of green and gold.

Family, Friends
and Fighting Back
Part 2

...I moved to Toronto when I was 18 years old to study nursing. It was an exciting time living away from home in the big city.

I graduated as a nurse from Sick Children's Hospital and worked for a year as a staff nurse.

This white nursing cap with the black stripe gave me a sense of pride and confidence, but I knew after a year as a staff nurse that I wanted more responsibility and decided to return to school.

I was pleased to be accepted in 1974 into the Nurse Practitioner program at McMaster University.

To get into the program the applicants had to have a doctor to sponsor them.

Not knowing any physicians in Toronto other than the residents in the hospital I referred to the yellow pages under Family Practitioners and started at "A" and by the time I got to "W" I was feeling tired and rather discouraged.

The first call to a "W" was the success I had been waiting for.

This physician accepted the offer and we entered the program together.

Sense of freedom

I was living an independent life with my own apartment and my own car. I felt like I had the world by the tail. I relished the freedom of independence.

Living under my parents roof worked when I was young but as an adolescent and young adult it hadn't afforded me the opportunity to make decisions for myself. I cherished this new independence.

It wasn't long after graduating from McMaster that I met Marc, a 24 yr old chemical engineer.

We were standing in the same line at a German beer garden in Toronto. I was with a girlfriend and he was behind us in the line.

He paid the host for a seat next to us.

I was with a girlfriend and was not looking to meet any fellows that evening, but we did end up sitting together and enjoyed each other's company.

We continued our relationship all that summer and in December we decided to marry.

He was going away to school in Quebec and I had grown so fond of his company that I was unwilling to stay behind.

Married, with children

We started our family within two years we were blessed with three beautiful children, one girl and two boys.

I was a devoted mother, but nursing was also a big part of my life.

I worked mostly part time evenings at the hospital so that Marc could be home with the kids. I loved nursing. It defined who I was and no matter where we lived it was easy for me to find work.

This was very important because during our twenty-five years of marriage we moved often. These were big moves, usually out of province and all related to a job change for Marc.

It was stressful but really it was the only stress we had in our lives. We were well suited, and very committed to each other, our children and, of course, our marriage.

One of our favorite experiences was living in Calgary. We had moved to Alberta for the second time in 1990 and happily adopted once again the western style of living.

The kids were 5, 10 and 13 years old, the perfect time in their life to enjoy the casual, relaxed lifestyle and Calgary's cowboy mentality.

The Calgary Stampede was a world class event that we celebrated every year along with thousands of other enthusiasts.

The five of us would get up at five o'clock the morning of the Stampede parade and head downtown with our friends to reserve our place at the curbside. The men elected to pick up coffee and donuts while we guarded the sacred spot at the parade site with our kids. It was a wonderful tradition and we always had front row seats!

Horsing around

It was on one of our visits to the Stampede that influenced us to buy two beautiful Peruvian Paso horses. One, a five year old liver chestnut mare, Eva, as sweet as any horse could be and the other, a big chestnut gelding, Bert, emotional and silly, but fun to ride. These were gaited Spanish horses considered in horse circles as the "Cadillac of riding horses." The mare was perfect for me as I had undergone extensive back surgery in May of '96.

The ride was smooth. There was no up and down movement, and because of both the gentle rhythm and her kind disposition, it was safe for me to ride. I desperately wanted to learn how to handle and ride horses but I realized as we started to spend more time with them that I was afraid of them.

Our riding instructor said to me one day when I was having a confidence problem: "Elizabeth these horses aren't predators. You just need to understand their mentality and you will understand their behavior. You are their leader."

I couldn't quite believe the "leader" thing.

Marc didn't have any fear of them and I often wished I could share his confidence. I knew how badly you could get hurt by a horse. I had gone to horse camp when I was twelve and watched a barn-hand get kicked by a horse - both feet, a kick that sent him flying through the air and landed him in hospital.

Over a six month time period, I slowly developed a relationship with the mare, and started to trust her and my abilities.

Part of the reason for my fear was my physical limitation. My limp and poor balance from the back surgery made me feel vulnerable. I looked to this horse as my teacher. We brought these two beautiful horses with us when we moved to Ontario, as well as our two dogs and two cats.

Back injury takes its toll

It was May of '97. I was still walking with a limp that I was told was due to the spinal cord injury from Nov '95 and subsequent surgery of May '96. I had gone through a difficult time emotionally, feeling quite insecure about my gait and the fact that I needed to walk with a cane. I felt disabled and ungainly and feared for my job. An emergency room nurse needs to hustle and at times run. I was not able to do this anymore.

My feet often felt like they didn't want to move. It was frustrating to not have the natural rhythm of movement that I had once taken for granted, but I was learning to live with it, and riding my horse gave me back the rhythm and grace that I had lost.

I was advised by the neurosurgeon when we left Calgary that I should be followed by a neurologist in Ontario and that I would benefit from some rehabilitation regarding my walking. Little did I know that this follow up in Ontario would be the beginning of the end, literally.

It was mid November and we had only been in Ontario for four months. This was move number nine and the five of us were trying to get used to our new surroundings.

Tired from the stress of the move and overwhelmed with the thought of serious health issues, Marc and I sat in a little blue room at the Medical Centre and waited for the second neurologist to arrive, an ALS specialist.

Diagnosed with ALS

I had seen another neurologist that day who had done all the tests and told us he wanted a final opinion to support his findings.

We knew what he suspected but we seemed to be walking in a dreamworld unsure of the meaning of the letters ALS and feeling solely dependant for support on this last doctor.

He came in and introduced himself. As he faced me checking my reflexes, I said to him with an air of apology, "I'm nervous." He replied "I know." I answered "I'm nervous of what you represent" feeling the need to make myself crystal clear and wanting reassurance. He didn't continued to test my reflexes.

After taking a thorough medical history that had become very complicated over the past three years, and at the end of the examination, he told us what we had both feared. "It is quite certain you have ALS."

When I asked him how long I had to live, he stated: "You will have to return in a month and I will know then how fast the disease is progressing. I suspect it will be the average time, two to five years."

All I knew of ALS was Sue Rodriguez and I felt a cold hard knot in the pit of my stomach.

It seemed so unreal. My thoughts were frantic. These things happened to other people. I was a nurse not a patient. I helped heal people. I could always fix things in my life, there was always a solution. That's what I had believed.

The doctor told us he needed to make some follow up arrangements and left the room.

Shock of Lou Gehrig's Disease

Marc was sitting on a wooden chair against the wall to my right and I was still sitting on the examination table, there were no words spoken.

After I got dressed we found our way down the long corridor to the neurology unit. We were introduced to the secretary and the kinesiologist who worked with the doctor in the research clinic.

I numbly smiled and said "hello" politely. I remember feeling like I was being initiated into an exclusive club, where only special members were allowed; all the staff knowing the reality that you didn't yet realize.

I remember the kinesiologist sitting beside me saying: "Just take it one day at a time." Little did I know that her suggestion would be very hard to accommodate for a long, long while.

Marc and I left the hospital holding hands. The ride home was silent.

Trees, blacktop and cars rushed past us in a blur. There was nothing to say. There were so many questions and no answers.

When we arrived in the safety and comfort of

our home we went to the internet for reassurance and information. Very quickly and with mounting sadness we learned all there was to know about ALS a rapid, progressive, fatal, neuromuscular disease that would cause paralysis of my arms, legs, speech and breathing muscles.

I could be thankful that it would not affect my brain or five senses but would leave me unable to communicate or express myself, unable to eat or breathe. There was no treatment and no cure.

One phrase I'll never forget described the ALS patient as a "a live body in a glass coffin."

How to tell the children?

I was so claustrophobic. How were we to deal with this? How were we to tell the children?

It was horrifying. I was so frightened. I would sit on the little built-in seat in our shower and cry endlessly. The noise of the shower drowned out the sound of my weeping.

After living with the news for a month I knew we had to tell the children.

They knew by our demeanor that there was something going on.

My eyes were often red from crying and they heard me up walking at night.

Our daughter, Renee was nineteen, and our sons Philippe and Andre were seventeen and twelve.

Moving to Ontario had brought us closer to my family, a sister and brother and their families and my mother and father.

They lived nearby. It was hard for them too. They knew what my diagnosis was and wanted to visit but felt uncomfortable hiding such a grave secret from the children. It was just four days before Christmas.

Marc and I asked the kids to come into the kitchen that evening and sit down. They had been through this scenario before, each time we told them we were moving.

They looked at us with the same anxious expectation. If only it had been that easy. I told them I was sick and wasn't going to get better.

Two of the children smiled. My daughter looked at her father, "that's not funny Papa." He was always playing tricks on them and they thought this was another way of being silly. They saw in my face however, that this wasn't "silly." I couldn't hold back the tears as I told them it would be all right and that we still had lots of fun times left.

News hits children hard

One asked how long I had. I told them two to five years but some people live longer.

They got up and left the table. How do you console your children after telling them something like this? Is there a right way or a wrong way to tell them? How do you protect them as you have always done? It was agonizing. I felt totally at a loss.

Marc and I continued to sit at the table for a long while. There was no sound to be heard except for the quiet, easy respirations of our two dogs. I needed to search out my youngest, Andre.

I walked upstairs, my cane tapped lightly on each step. I found him lying on the floor of the loft crying. I lay down beside him and curled my body around his.

With halting words I whispered: "It will be OK honey." I knew in my heart it wouldn't be OK and

I knew nothing would ever be the same again.

Over the next few months we functioned as a normal family.

Christmas came and went. Easter dinner boasted a full table of family members, uncles, aunts, cousins and Nana and Grandad.

Nothing was spoken of my illness it was like a big white elephant was in the room that everyone saw but no one acknowledged.

As a family we seemed to be coping. The kids seemed more connected to each other and I could feel their concern for me.

They made me cups of tea and carried my plate to the supper table. They helped me up off the floor when I would fall.

Sleepless nights

There was more laughter in the house than there had ever been. The only outward sign of anything having changed was my sleeplessness.

Panic would drive me from our comfortable double bed that had always been a safe, warm retreat.

As quietly as was possible with my staggering gait I would get up sometime after midnight and sit in my leather chair in the living room, the hot cup of tea, familiar and comforting.

I visited the specialist every month for the next year and started a study drug. It was a blind study so no one knew what they were on, if anything.

I could now feel increasing weakness and I knew I was losing a little more of myself every day.

I was walking with a walker and my speech was sounding more hoarse.

I could not swallow bread or meat very easily

and I was slightly short of breath when lying down.

At night my hips and shoulder joints ached from the pressure of partially dead weight and my knees resting on each other when I was lying on my side. The spasms in my legs would often wake me from fitful dreams, dreams of being buried alive.

I moaned and talked in the night and would frequently scream in my sleep.

Marc had learned to wake me gently before the crescendo of the nightmare.

Thinking about death

I functioned well during the light of day and carried on with my life but I thought about death often.

I found it difficult to talk to my own doctor about my feelings on the end of life issues and he didn't agree with my philosophy.

He told me to trust him. He told me that in all his experience with this disease, he found that the less people had the more they wanted to live.

I felt it was easy for him to feel that life had value right up until the end, he was not going to end up paralyzed and unable to communicate.

I remember asking him how he would want to die if he had ALS?

He said "I would like to die on the top of a mountain."

I replied "you would have to first be able to climb the mountain." He didn't answer.

Six months after my diagnosis, I sought out a palliative care specialist, looking for reassurance but I found she too was unable to reassure me or to promise me help in the end; to die with dignity. She was a good listener but gave me the same professional response that to me was so unsatisfying as it skirted the issues.

I have been working in the medical system and with health professionals long enough to know these are the responses that doctors give to patients but I still didn't feel like a patient I wanted to be treated like a colleague with the same respect and honesty that any medical person should and could expect.

The difference between myself and other patients was that I was perfectly aware of what was now happening and what was going to happen to me during this illness. I really didn't need a doctor; the disease would take me anyway.

All the doctor was doing was monitoring my decline. I could do that better than he could, I believed. The only thing the doctor had that I didn't was the power to write a prescription. I was determined to settle the issue of my death before I became totally incapacitated.

Contemplating suicide

While returning home from dropping my son off at hockey one spring morning, I drove into the garage and sat there listening to Kenny Rogers singing "I Will Remember You" on the tape. I had been crying hard all the way home.

My life was so out of control. I was going to die. I didn't want my children or family to see me in a totally dependent state, I wasn't sure if I could handle the loss of dignity. I felt so fearful.

I closed the garage door and let the car run. It was so easy and so comfortable. I remember thinking, if this was depression it was helping me to do the one thing that I was so afraid of. I was glad it was so easy.

But it was not time yet. I turned the car off. I

knew I was still able to give to my family and I had to find out if Marc would be angry with me for doing this. I needed some support on this journey.

One night, a few days later, I told him what I had done and asked him what he'd do.

He said he would support me in what ever I chose to do, but he also made it very clear that he could not assist me with my death.

I felt relieved that I still seemed to have the option of sitting in the car.

Writing poetry

At nighttime, not long after that I began to write poetry. I would get up after everyone was asleep and make a cup of tea in the kitchen.

Placing the mug carefully on my walker I would wind my way around the sleepy dogs and settle in my chair in the corner of the living room.

These were some of my darkest hours. The house was quiet and the lamplight was soft.

The animals were quite happy to have company. One of the cats, Mocha quickly found her place by my side.

I would sit in my leather chair wrapped in the maroon wool blanket my mother had made for me the Christmas before and sip my tea.

My thoughts were clear and the words flowed from the pen effortlessly.

I could speak my fears and truths privately, expressing them in my poems.

The rhyme of the poetry seemed to have an innocence and whimsy that made me feel connected once again to a childhood that had offered me a safe place and an easy, uncomplicated life. The rhythm of the words was my only comfort.

How had my life so drastically changed in such a short space of time?

In these quiet hours I also started making deals with God. I begged and pleaded. I asked for forgiveness and I asked him to give me ways to help myself. He didn't seem to be listening.

I had spent so many years of my life helping people and always being concerned for others feelings and welfare. I heard the words "she's a pleaser."

How could that be such a bad thing? Wasn't life about giving and making others happy? Maybe I had it all wrong.

Searching for a legacy

The other issue that haunted me continually was what my legacy would be to the world.

Death was so final, so very final. I had fears about being forgotten, being a nothing, a nobody.

I wasn't a painter who could paint a masterpiece and I didn't know how to write a book.

I was even afraid that after my death my children would forget what I looked like reminded only with the help of old photographs.

A friend gave me a Christmas gift on the second Christmas after my diagnosis. It was a small bird's nest. In it were three golden eggs.

I knew what my legacy was and I understood what she was telling me.

I knew I would always live on through my children but it wasn't enough.

It couldn't satisfy a deeper need I had to make a difference while I was still able.

There had to be something I could do for

others who were suffering with this horrible illness.

It was so hard to explain the burning desire I had reach out to the world around me – I needed them to listen I needed them to hear. I truly understood how isolating this disease was and wanted to make my point loud and clear.

I considered standing on the top of the CN tower to draw attention to this nightmarish illness and even more seriously, considered riding across Canada on a scooter from Newfoundland to Vancouver, but realized that with my deteriorating condition I couldn't possibly make it.

I was also discouraged strongly by my family, a reaction that hurt me very much. They were very concerned for me and for my health.

My father worried that I would not be understood and my efforts would fall flat in the public eye.

I was hurt and angry. I felt they really didn't understand.

"Laugh, I thought I'd die"

In the fall of '99 I reread the book "Laugh, I thought I'd Die" by Dennis Kaye and it proved to be inspiring.

Kaye was a young man who was diagnosed with ALS at the age of twenty-eight. He had a truly wonderful wife and three lovely young children. He was an optimist and a tremendously funny man.

He wrote funny letters to Peter Gzowski describing what it was like to live with this disease.

Kaye jokingly called himself " The Incredible Shrinking Man". The letters were read over CBC Radio's Morningside program.

I started to believe that if he could make a

positive thing out of this terrible situation then I could rise to the same challenge. I knew I had to work with the overwhelming passion I was feeling.

My strength had always been in talking to people and winning their friendship. I knew I would be able to reach the prominent people.

Sending out a message

I wanted to not only send my message to the public to increase the awareness of this hidden illness, but I also wanted to find a way to make a difference that would be remembered long after I was gone.

I wanted to organize a benefit concert with numerous popular artists.

I imagined organizing a concert similar to the benefit that was done for African famine relief, "Tears Are Not Enough" where all the well known Canadian artists came together to sing for the cause.

This would be my legacy.

I sat down at my computer and started to write letters. I believed for every ten "No's" I would get one "Yes." I needed the help of the big voices.

We would simply have to raise the profile of this disease if we were ever to find a treatment… (continued in Part 3 after the following selection of poems).

Poems
Learning Life's Lesson

Elizabeth Grandbois, February 2000:
I have realized in these past two years how much I took my life and my health for granted.

Life's Lesson

Lost without a future,
still learning how to cope,
promises of healing
leave little room for hope.
The details of my life,
are governed now by time,
luxuries of dreaming
all but left behind.
Locked into this destiny
I'm powerless to change,
accepting the reality
is fraught with deepest pain.
I'm reminded of the freedom,
of life that was before,
consoled by tender memories,
but wanting so much more.
Tomorrow was a surety,
it always came again,
I took it all for granted,
my confidence was vain.

Elizabeth Grandbois, November 1999:
At one point, I seriously considered ending my life.

Are You Listening

The choice I make to end my life
is not to do with pride,
but all about my dignity
and fear.
I do believe I have the right
to take the final say,
death will come regardless,
in a more invasive way.
Grieving goes along with death,
it will remain the same,
there is no one to blame.
I truly hope you never feel
the sorrow that I hide,
it grabs you soul,
it tears your heart,
… so far removed from pride.

Elizabeth Grandbois, July 2002: This is a treasured memory that I allow to flow through my mind…

Peace on the Water

*We venture out at sunrise, before the seagulls wake
steering our canoe as we glide along the shore,
swirling mist is lifted by the warmth of early sun,
the rhythm of our paddles
breaks the stillness of the morn.*

*We dip and pull our way across a shimmering lake
as streams of crystal water spill from polished oars,
the cool, tiny droplets break the calm of liquid glass,
teasing hungry sunfish that surface for a meal.*

*In a moment of humility we lay our paddles down
savouring all simplicity of water, wind and air,
Bathed in tranquility, we clear our brimming minds,
surrendering to nature and the current's gentle lure.*

Elizabeth Grandbois, May 2002: A good friend is like an old pair of slippers, comforting and dependable.

A Notion, Slippers and Friends

*You are a friend to me
like slippers that mould to brittle feet,
you cushion the hurt, and warm the weary sole.
You have followed my journey,
enduring the strain
while securing the spring in my step.
You have kept pace with my spirit
and tended my fragility.
Now, what can I give you in return?*

Elizabeth Grandbois, November 1999:
My husband is my comfort…

Together

We are together.
Wine glasses sparkle in the firelight,
shadows flicker on the wall
dancing to the music.
I feel your warmth,
our fingers entwine.
Gently, briefly, we kiss.
Bound by intimacy,
love is our secret.

Elizabeth Grandbois, August 1999: I recall little Philippe at the hockey arena...

The Goalie

A pungent odour filled the air
a sea of blue and white,
as boys donned pads and helmets
for their hockey game that night.
The goalie lay face to the floor
as if a monk in prayer,
"Do my pads up! Hurry Dad!
There's not much time to spare."
He stood and put his helmet on
pulled the chin strap tight,
he grabbed his stick, pushed through the door
and disappeared from sight.
How strange to see this little boy
standing with his mates,
bigger with his leather pads,
taller with his skates.
He skated to the empty net
stretching on the way,
he took his place inside the crease
and waited for the play.
Then, before the puck was dropped
a thought came to the lad,
he turned, he smiled, raised his hand
and waved to Mum and Dad.

Elizabeth Grandbois, February 2002: My father has long been a source of strength and inspiration…

Essence Of My Father

Striding confidently along the promenade,
he leans forward,
slightly,
shoulders to the wind,
his pace decidedly purposeful.
Ninety years,
a slim, solitary silhouette,
outlined
against the still morning waters
of Lake Ontario.
While the world sleeps
the birds circle,
he is never alone.
He pauses
to wonder at the bright blazing sun, radiant on the horizon
then turns
and gently extends his palm to the full, pale moon setting behind.
He reflects,
 "Here, you see the Power and the Glory."
What I really see,
is the magnificence of life,
and the depth of my father's soul.

Elizabeth Grandbois, November 1999:
The doctor couldn't help me...

Game of Life

He sits there in his favoured chair
asks how I feel,
in all his wisdom and his want
he's powerless to heal.
His kind words hold no comfort
for one who feels such grief,
his professional sincerity
offers no relief.
Turn and look me in the eye,
tell me what you see,
are you burdened by your knowledge
or saddened like me.
I am not the only one
who's losing at this game,
you know all their names...

Elizabeth Grandbois, November 1999:
I worried that time was passing too fast.

Seasons

Leaves have fallen, days are short,
summer slips away,
where have all the hours gone.
Festive celebrations mark another season's end,
fragrant golden turkey
shared with family and friends.
Pumpkin faces once aglow
are nipped by early frost,
while gaily colored costumes
now lie folded in a box.
I watch as crystal flakes of snow
softly touch the ground,
in contrast to crackling leaves
they fall without a sound.
This dormant scene before me,
a pristine winter white
will soon become a wonderland
of sparkling Christmas light.
The passing of these seasons
lends joy to sweet recall,
honouring such old traditions,
winter, spring and fall.

Reaching Heaven

*Give me wings to fly away beyond the steel blue sky,
let go the sorrow and tears.
I float through cotton clouds, the wind across my face
I have reached the hallowed place.
Spirit voices sing to me in languages untold,
gentle arms envelop me and draw me to the fold.
Golden star lights flicker, I make my final wish,
forgiveness everlasting.*

Disquiet of Doubt

*In a moment of strength I have revealed myself
in my weakness I am alone.
Without ending, the passion grows weary,
uniqueness becomes familiar
and inspiration seems foolish,
to the world
or just to me?*

God

*Are you listening,
do you hear me
when I call your name in prayer,
are you watching,
do you see me
in my moments of despair,
are you out there,
can you sense me
when I'm searching for a sign,
will I ever have the answer?
Are you magic,
are you mystic,
can you turn the clock around,
are you ghostly,
are you hidden,
will you let yourself be found,
are you real,
are you existent,
do you represent the truth,
will I ever get to know you,
will it do me any good?
With your wisdom
and your power
is it worth my while to hope,
with your kindness
and your glory
can you help my faith to grow,
will you share
or can you show me
just a little of your grace,
that I can be more peaceful?*

Elizabeth Grandbois, January 2000: When life seems darkest, I like to write…

A Life In Ink

When the day is at its longest
and my mood is less than bright,
I put my pen to paper.
I feel emotions stir,
a passion fills my mind,
the words come tumbling to the page
and fall in line by line.
Their rhythm gives comfort
like an old familiar song,
the thoughts flow out in measured form
as from the pen they're drawn.
These words give meaning to my life,
the verse keeps me alive,
when the pen no longer speaks
I fear my soul will die.
If my soul should pass away,
my poems will live on,
and I pray I'll be remembered
like the lyrics of a song.

Elizabeth Grandbois, Feb. 2000: The baby's parents had refused treatment. It was my first year of nursing.

Little Lamb

It was night time on the infant ward
the halls were deathly still,
through the cloak of silence
I heard the tiny wail.
I turned, listened, slipped down from the stool
then followed the sound
to the far end of the hall.
*The sign said **"Do Not Feed"** with a great black mark,*
I opened up the door
and stepped into the dark.
Through the window shone the moonlight,
I saw the metal crib,
hearing muffled whimpers,
I walked over to the bed.
There he was a little babe bundled in a sheet,
an IV taped upon his head,
his weakened cry, a bleat.
I reached down very tenderly
and took him in my arms,
he was lighter than a feather,
his body barely warm.
I sat down in the rocker,
reminded not to feed,
I placed a soother in his mouth to pacify his need.
My tears fell on his silky head,
I hummed a cradle song,
I knew that before sunrise this baby would be gone.
Throughout the years my thoughts return
to that night on the ward,
to my dear little friend I had the privilege to hold.

Elizabeth Grandbois, August 1999:
I wrote the poem Timeless Love when I was thinking of the stages of our marriage.

Timeless Love

Will you love me love of mine
when babies cry at night,
and pull me from our soft warm bed.
from arms that hold me tight.
And will you love me dearest one
when work demands are great,
when others need you more than I.
Will you be there with me
when relatives abide,
cocooning me with endless love
and pressing you aside.
Can I trust that you'll protect me
when illness makes me weak,
when I am bent and paralyzed,
and cannot speak.
Will your love be my salvation,
until the very end,
this we'll only know in time,
… my lover and my friend.

Finding Hope
Part 3

...I was alarmed to discover the death rate from ALS is comparable to the death rate from AIDS.

And I realized we were losing 2-3 Canadians a *day* to a disease of which **no one ever spoke**.

Funding to fight ALS was a fraction of what the other better known illnesses were receiving and financial costs often bankrupted families of victims.

I wrote to all the television networks and I wrote to the radio stations.

I sent my story to a national magazine, Canadian Living.

I also wrote to many artists asking them if they would be interested in participating in such a benefit concert. The responses started coming in.

The CBC news crew came into our home in March of 2000 and created a story about ALS and our family.

Telling story on national television

It was my first exposure to the media. It was more personal and sadder than I wanted it to be but it covered all the important points, the statistics and the horror of the disease.

Early one morning, they arrived at our door with the cameraman and a load of equipment.

The person organizing the taping was petite. She looked different that she did on the television.

Unlike her professional look for the evening news, she wore no make-up. She had on jeans and a checkered shirt, her blonde hair tied up in a casual ponytail.

Her smile was warm and her manner friendly. She explained that we would be working at this all day.

The kids had taken the day off of school and were excited about what would be happening. It turned out to be a very long, tiring, emotional day.

We had to repeat mechanical movements for the cameraman eight to ten times until they felt the angle and details were perfect.

They altered the lighting and rearranged our furniture. The whole scene looked so disorganized.

Our usually quite orderly house was hardly recognizable. The piece, as we were to understand later was a collage of family life captured in bits and pieces and put together to create a story.

In the afternoon the personal interviews started. I was comfortable talking about the disease, but it took the kids and Marc off guard. They were not used to talking about their feelings and the questions were personal.

She reassured all of us that we should just answer as best we could, whatever we were comfortable answering. The interviews were private so we didn't hear the other family member's remarks, but I knew the kids were upset. They felt their personal thoughts were being exposed, but on the other hand, they knew how important this was to me. We had discussed the possible loss of privacy when I started writing my letters.

By 7 pm the crew, were finished and set to leave. I met them the next day at the Medical Centre and the filming continued in the clinical setting. It was over by late afternoon.

Nation-wide campaign begins

This was the beginning of my campaign. Canada AM promised me a spot in June 2000 for ALS awareness month.

I received letters and phone calls from famous Canadian broadcasters Pamela Wallen and Vicki Gabereau. They were both interested in my story.

Then, one afternoon, in April while the children were at school and Marc was at work, the occupational therapist and a woman from Homecare came to measure me for my wheelchair.

With my deterioration it was evident that I would probably need one in the next six months and I was advised to go ahead and order it as it usually took quite a number of months to get it after placing the order.

I was also told that I should order the deluxe model with tilt ability that would accommodate the puff and sniff adaptations for when I was unable to use my hands. These were the realities I was facing.

The white van arrived in the driveway and from behind the sheer curtain I anxiously watched them unload the heavy chair.

Wheelchair 'monster' arrives

Reluctantly I opened the door wide and forced myself to smile. They wheeled the largest looking black monster up the ramp and onto the front step.

The Homecare woman was having difficulty driving it over the threshold and the two of them were somewhat amused with her trials.

At that moment I wanted to disappear. It felt like an invasion. I was outnumbered, three against one, and I really didn't want them here. Dear God, this was awful.

The chair was a big, ugly, cumbersome thing made of black steel. She drove it into the living room showing me how easily it pivoted on the spot. She climbed out of the chair and pointed to all the features.

The occupational therapist looked at me and asked me if I'd like to try sitting in it.

When I said "No" she looked slightly surprised and then her face seemed to soften: "I understand, you don't have to right now."

I just wanted them to leave.

They asked me if I had any questions. They were obviously friends and left maneuvering the monster and talking about their own stuff.

I closed the door. It was just another slide down this slippery slope. I felt panicky, but I was determined not to cry.

Shortly after they left, Philippe my now nineteen year old son came home from school.

He was sitting at the table with his back to me eating his usual lumberjack snack.

I wanted to tell him about my day but was so afraid of worrying him.

I said quietly, "they came to measure me for my wheelchair today"

He turned and looked at me and stated quite emphatically, "That sucks!"

I was so relieved. He knew what I was feeling and couldn't have said it any better. I wheeled my walker over to the table and gave him a big hug. He was only a kid but he understood.

Telling story on national radio

In May, CBC radio invited me to tell my tale on "First Person Singular."

I had written my story and sent it on to the producer. She wrote back: "The story is good and has great potential. If you're up for a rewrite I'll help you."

She understood my goals of awareness and understanding, and reassured me that we would be able to get across the tragedy of the disease through the the telling of my story.

With great tact and diplomacy, she worked with me on the editing via email and within a week it was ready to be read on air. On the day of taping my sister Jennifer drove me down to the big CBC building, an institution supporting 3,000 employees.

It was a huge, gray building with red crosses on the outside that gave it a "Swiss" look.

All the floors were open to the centre of the building and looked down onto a central foyer.

Entering the media world

There were pictures of famous journalists and TV and radio personalities everywhere. We were met by a funny fellow in Bermuda shorts, a golf shirt and knee socks.

He introduced himself as Don "the official greeter," his manner was friendly and chatty as he ushered us to the taping studio where I was to meet the producer.

The area where we waited was filled with half walls separating the different work stations. The CBC radio show was being piped in the background.

Within minutes she arrived. As always, when you have had a relationship with someone but have never seen them, it's always surprising when you meet. I had pictured her differently in my mind.

I imagined her to be tall and very sophisticated, but she was casually dressed, pretty in a natural sort of way with medium length, dark brown hair. Her smile put me at ease immediately.

She led me to the taping room and showed me where to sit. It was a dimly lit room with a large, round, black table in the center.

I was to sit at the table in front of a microphone that was supported on a long metal arm.

She explained how I was to read the story and if I had to stop, to be sure to stop at the end of a sentence and pause. This would allow them to cut and tape without losing any of the story.

They closed the door and left me on my own. Straight ahead was a glass window where my sister Jennifer, the producer and the two technicians sat. I heard her say "anytime you're ready Elizabeth."

I started reading but after the first three sentences, out of the corner of my eye I could see movement behind the window. I looked up to see, my sister making the hand signal of "time out."

The radio people looked at her with surprised expressions.

She said "we need a camera. How often do you get to come to the CBC and read a story on the radio?" They left to hunt down a camera.

When they returned they had a tiny little instamatic that produced pictures the size of your thumb that you could stick on cards. They seemed to be quite amused.

Jennifer snapped three or four pictures. They left me alone again and resumed their places behind the window. Again I heard "whenever you're ready Elizabeth, just continue where you left off."

I started the story over again. After I finished my story, the producer came into the room and told me I had done an excellent job. She asked me to keep in touch. I was amazed at the response and support I was getting from the outside world.

Public speaking tours begin

The next opportunity was an invitation to speak to Rotary in my hometown. This was my first time speaking in public and I knew there would be at least 65 businessmen and women attending.

My friend Rob said this would be a good group to concentrate on, as Rotarians were always willing to help a good cause.

The morning arrived. This was my first public address. I invited my doctor to come and support what I had to say about this disease.

I stood there at the podium looking into a sea of faces.

I was surprised at my lack of anxiety in front of all these people. I told them my story.

When I was finished, my doctor stood up. He started speaking about the hopelessness of this illness and the disastrous funding afforded by government.

Doctor tells of new 'ALS' treatment

My doctor then told a story that he had recently read in a Neurology journal about a 38 yr old woman who had AIDS and was subsequently diagnosed with ALS.

She deteriorated very rapidly to a bedridden state having to be fed with a tube, unable to move.

The doctors decided to treat her AIDS infection and within 6 months she was up walking unassisted and her ALS symptoms had disappeared.

I can't remember what he said after that. I was so stunned by the story he had just told.

He sat down at the table and before I had a chance to comment, the meeting was over and he had left for the hospital.

I called him that day and the next two days and left messages that I wanted to take the AIDS drugs. I didn't hear from him until the next week.

It was the longest five days of my life.

He was concerned about the cost and that it

could make me very sick. The drugs could damage my liver and I would not be eligible for a transplant.

His comments did not make much sense to me. I was already dying and I would rather go from liver disease than ALS. At least with liver disease I would probably lose my mind. And it didn't matter how much it cost. We'd sell the house for a second chance at life.

Waiver signed to start AIDS treatment

The doctor told me we would have to sign a waiver if I wanted this treatment. I signed the day before I was to leave for Calgary to visit old friends.

I wanted to cancel the trip so I could start the drugs right away, but I knew it would disappoint too many people.

The trip to Calgary had been planned for a long time. It was actually a six day business trip for Marc that offered me an opportunity to visit all my friends. It would be the last time I would see them as my condition was on a downhill slide.

It would be an emotional visit. I was having difficulty swallowing and sometimes choked on food.

My voice was weak and croaky most of the time. My walking was so slow and labored now and it was a tremendous effort to go anywhere. My lower legs swelled so badly and became so discoloured when I was sitting for long periods. I used wheelchairs in the airport as the walk to the plane was too far for me.

Even while sitting on the plane I was having difficulty opening the plastic wrap on my utensils.

We arrived at the Bow Valley Hotel and settled into our hotel room. Early the next morning we drove out to Acme, to the ranch where, the summer before, we had shipped my mare, Eva and her filly, Novia.

I wasn't able to ride anymore as I had lost all my leg power and we felt our friend and breeder, Mimi would be able to sell them quite easily for us. I hadn't seen Eva for a year and she hadn't sold. I knew this would be the last time I would see her as well.

When we arrived at the ranch I noticed the red trailer sitting in front of the barn. It was Marc's cousin's truck and trailer from Quebec! I didn't understand why it was there. This was such a long way from home for them.

Birthday surprise

Marc walked over to the trailer and shook his cousin's hand. They turned and smiled at me. It was two days before my birthday and they had made plans to surprise me by bringing my mare home.

The owner of the ranch, Mimi brought Eva out of the paddock. She was covered in dried mud and I knew she had been rolling in it to relieve the irritation of the flies. She was not a pretty sight.

I wheeled my walker towards her, brushing away my tears. I called her name. She turned her head and looked at me. It was such a thrill to see her again. I hugged her, holding onto her mane to keep my balance. She nuzzled my pockets looking for cookies. She smelled so good, she smelled like Eva. I watched them load her onto the trailer. She was going home.

My emotions were mixed. I felt happy and excited, but at the same time felt tremendous sadness for what I was losing and what I had already lost.

I really wanted to just go home not only to start the drugs, but now to be with my mare again, even if it was just to look at her... (to be continued in Part 4 after the following selection of poetry)

Poems
Shared Moments of Life

Elizabeth Grandbois, August 1999: My daughter was still adjusting to the news of my illness…

Shared Moments

I wake up every morning and stumble from my bed,
the memory of illness slowly seeps into my head.
The day is new and fresh but senses feel so dull,
perhaps a cup of coffee….
I head to the kitchen with my walker for support,
there my sweet daughter prepares breakfast,
she smiles and asks how I'd like my bagel done today
"Just a little butter and only half of one."
She pours the coffee, brings the bread
and settles at her place,
shared, tender moments, remembrances of grace.

Elizabeth Grandbois, August 1999:
The second poem, A Child's Lament, was written on a day when I was thinking about my 12-year-old son's reaction to the news of my illness...

A Child's Lament

*What's happening to my mother
he asks himself one day,
she used to move so quickly
in a graceful sort of way.
She's tripping over both her feet
and bumping into doors,
she needs my hand to help her
as she gets up off the floor.
Her eyes are red from crying
when I come home from school,
I'm trying to understand
I know she has an illness,
and her legs are getting worse,
I'm not sure what to do,
or how to end this curse.
I hear her say she loves me
and I try to give her help,
but she just keeps on falling.
I wish that she would rest.
I don't know what will happen,
Still, if God can see my Mum,
I know that he'll look after her
...as I have done.*

Elizabeth Grandbois, April 2000:
Who will comfort me?

Secrets of the Heart

*Who will sing a lullaby
when spirits fail to sleep,
who will wish upon a star
for grieving souls who weep.*

*Who will seek a rainbow,
or find a pot of gold,
and who will ease foreboding,
when courage has grown cold.*

*Who will find a four leaf clover
barely new and green,
or reach to touch an angel,
then awaken from a dream.
I will sing at night time,
hum a lovely cradle song,
I'll watch for shooting stars
'til early hours of dawn.*

*I will catch the rainbow
when sun showers bring the rain,
then bathe myself in memories
to ease the deepest pain.*

*I'll walk through fields of clover
to find that lucky leaf,
and share it with the angel
who comforts me in sleep.*

Elizabeth Grandbois, November 2001: I love horses.

Wonder of Horses

*I can smell the fragrant leather
streaked with saddle soap,
we rubbed 'til the brown skin took a shine,
sitting in the tack room adorned with souvenirs
we worked on each harness, yours and mine.
The horses' reins soaked in the thick golden oil,
they gleamed as we hung them on the stand,
halters would be soft and supple by the morn
ready for the ride that we'd planned.
This finely crafted tack was sculptured in Peru,
chiselled in florid Spanish style,
we scrubbed with a brush to remove
old dirt and dust
then waxed the hide, conversing all the while.
Our horses came to greet us as the sun began to rise,
their dark hooves glistened in the dew,
with gleaming saddles strapped
over strong smooth backs,
we took to seasoned trails that we knew.
The flush of freedom warmed us,
we crossed farmer's fields,
head to tail and sometimes side by side,
spirits gently lulled by the rhythmic lilting gait
as our equine friends granted us a ride.
The deep, mysterious peace
that unites horse and man
offers testament to nature's quiet grace,
this power of communion
outside the mortal class
has revealed to me
an untold mystic place.*

Elizabeth Grandbois, April 2000:
I think animals do understand.

My "Torti" Cat

*My cat is as indifferent as any cat can be
but yesterday without demur,
she climbed upon my knee.
She coyly stretched out languidly
and looked me in the eye,
in gestures only known to cats,
she asked me why I cried.
She lay there waiting patiently
attentive to my pain,
then placed her paw against my chest,
as teardrops fell like rain.
She raised her head to watch my face
searching for a sign,
wanting me to comfort her
and tell her I was fine.
I knew my mourning worried her
but sadness ran too deep,
to reassure this anxious cat,
the reasons why I weep.
She gave me her companionship,
blinking eyes of gold,
expressing in her feline way,
that I was still her world.*

Elizabeth Grandbois, May 2000:
Planning ahead for my deteriorating state is so hard.

Mobile Monster

They are coming,
I'll cope.
I try to hang on,
it's a slippery slope.
I open the door and show them in,
they manoeuvre the monster,
three against one;
two with legs, one with four wheels,
big, black, powerful steel..
Where is my power?
Slipping away.
I know it will one day be part of my body,
part of my life,
but now I'm not ready.
I'm gracious, I thank them,
I close the door.
I close my eyes wanting to cry.
Hours slip away, a time to reflect
on this monster,
a symbol of ominous death.

Elizabeth Grandbois, April 2001:
I felt like I was living under a microscope.

Dark Dilemma

*I want to be my own man,
I want to feel I'm free,
I want to live my life again.
I hear it when they come around,
I hear it when they call,
I hear the worry in their words.
Tell me how she's feeling,
is there sadness in her voice,
maybe we should visit.*

*What's happened to my privilege,
how could it all have changed,
in such a painful space of time,
my life's been rearranged.
My world is in a slow reverse,
dwindling down in size,
I struggle with the fear
of a crippling demise.
I have no other choice
but to accept what has been given
finding ways to tolerate
this crumbling world I live in.*

Elizabeth Grandbois, June 2001:
I love to visit and tend the world that is my garden.

A Garden of Wonder

I tend my children.
They are the roses in my garden.

My firstborn brightly colored, is always in bloom,
she stands tall showing off her blossoms,
the rain never bends her petals.
My second, a quiet beauty,
unveils soft autumn colours,
flowers always the same in size and number,
his fragrance lingers as you pass by.
My third grows in all directions,
branches wind and twist,
the small white blossoms not yet mature.
I carefully prune and shape,
his new growth comes in stronger and more plentiful.

I carry them with me; waxed, pressed
and tenderly guarded between the pages of my mind.

Eyes

*If we cannot read another's mind,
how are we to understand.
It's in the eyes,
the gladness,
the sadness,
the truth.
If you do not want me to understand
then close your eyes.*

The Visitor

*Speak to me softly, for I can hear the words
e'en though I cannot make a sound,
look into my eyes, that I can see your soul
where reassuring truths can still be found.
Touch me gently when you're near,
stroke my tired hand, I feel so burdensome today,
talk warmly of the past, engage me once again
comfort me before you go away.*

Elizabeth Grandbois, September 2001:
Some images will be burned forever into our collective memories.

After The Sleep
(Sept. 11, '01)

Today the world wakened to its own mortality.

Have we been fooled by the notion
  that we have control over our destiny,
an innate belief in our own power
  that enables us to look at our future with naïve confidence?

The walls around us, falsely secure
  have blinded us to the need for human interaction,
    the solace that comes from belonging.

If we are to survive we must embrace life,
  seek the humanity in one another
    by opening our hearts and our doors,

*only then will we share the vision **not** the certainty of a tomorrow.*

Elizabeth Grandbois, October 2001:
Fear, fury and frustration were everywhere…

The Price of Freedom

*We search for the enemy
in each and every face,
within our countries borders
all around.
The armies are positioned
preparing for a fight,
against the very devil they can't find.*

*Civilians try to hide
from destruction yet to come,
fearful for the children that they love.
Many there before
survived a fruitless war,
knowing that it never could be won.*

*What will be our fate
in this very caustic fight,
what signs justify the call;
can the innocents understand
that we must protect our land,
righteously defending who we are.*

*We have targeted the villain
with unforgiving force
desperate to be free of all we fear.
Such wreckage we disclaim
will bring us bitter shame
denying any honour in this war.*

Alone

Living in solitude,
thoughts unheard,
feelings untouched.
Life goes on
without me.
I am not gone yet.
I try to be there.
There is no connection.
The pain is in dying,
not in death.

Life's Flame

Released from death's embrace
I am delivered
from the cloying, choking feeling
that buried me in sleep.
The shroud of fear is lifted
as life's flame
chases the shadow of darkness
... still lurking at my back.

Elizabeth Grandbois, November 2001:
Lost, then found…

Lost Soul

I weep for my boy, wistful and shy,
for the scent of fresh air on fine flaxen hair
and worn little shoes askew on the stair,
for art work, and hockey sticks.
I weep for this young man
lured to the snare
of powdery, poisonous rapture.
I cry for his lost soul
my now distant son.
I cry for my own soul.
The rain is falling,
the sky is crying
for me
and for my boy.

Elizabeth Grandbois, November 2001:
At times, silence is deafening.

Blight of Silence

*Devoured by silence,
hung up by loss
that I cannot wash,
swallow,
or sleep away;
defeated by fate
and the abrasive truth
of blank faces
that attend all
but say little.
I am crumbling,
speak to me
you players
indifferent to the deadlock.*

Elizabeth Grandbois, September 1999:
One of the most difficult days for me was the day I sent my mare back to Calgary.

The Gift

Carry me through the forest
as leaves crackle beneath your feet,
gait smoothly my chestnut mare,
let the rocking motion soothe my grief.
Give me your strength
know my heart yearns to follow,
walk on through the cedar grove,
let sweet fragrance calm my sorrow.
You have given me freedom,
you have given me joy,
you are my teacher,
you are a gift,
but now,
you are gone.

Elizabeth Grandbois, November 2001:
Do you ever have one of those mornings when you just don't feel like getting out of bed?

Comfort under Cover

*Bleak November days, colourless and drab
lend a heaviness here inside my soul,
my self indulgent sense says pull the covers up,
the day is grey and winds are blowing cold.*

*Faded autumn leaves whirl wildly in the yard,
their parent twigs stark against the sky,
these warm woollen blankets embrace me like a friend,
they call me to stay here as I lie.*

*The corners of the window panes are sweating,
I ask myself who sweats when it's so cold,
maybe mother nature will forgo the wintry freeze,
there's a whisper Jack Frost has grown too old.*

*With the day just barely new, I'll lie a little more
savouring the comfort of my bed,
I'll plan a lovely daydream as I fall back to sleep
and slumber with these musings in my head.*

In Dreams
Part 4

...Marc is so very thoughtful and I realize how much I treasure every moment I can spend with him.

The next few days are spent visiting old Calgary friends. They came to the hotel one after another. By the second day, the young intuitive waitress in the coffee emporium understood that my friends were going to continue to come for the week, and so every morning after Marc and I finished our breakfast, she would put a "reserved" sign on the table by the window for me.

The friends came and went. We talked about old times and shared our feelings. They were weepy, and they cried for me. I was living with this illness every day so I was used to the reality, but my decline was shocking to them and they shed their tears for what was now visible to them. I didn't feel weepy.

For me, there were no more tears to cry. It was difficult going over it all with each friend, the fears and trials of the disease, but they were such good people and so genuinely interested in what I was experiencing.

I truly loved them and what they had meant to me over the years. I felt lonely now that we lived in the east. I only had one longtime friend and some new acquaintances, but it wasn't the same.

It didn't feel like home. I felt very alone even with my loving family surrounding me. I was used to my own independence.

A gathering of friends

On the Wednesday evening during our stay in Calgary, my friend Marie invited us to her home for dinner. Her husband, Johann picked me up in front of the hotel at 5:30 pm.

Marc was to meet us at the house at 6 pm. Johann was on time and I was delighted to see him again. He and Marc used to have such a good time in the hockey arenas when our boys were playing hockey. They would yell "Homer" at the referees when they didn't like the call. Those were good years. Johann and I chatted about the old, hockey times all the way to Parkland. Here, he pulled into the Community Centre.

I wasn't sure why we were stopping until I saw Marie, Les and Nancy, all my good friends standing at the door. They were coming out to greet me. Suddenly I understood. This was a gathering for me. They pinned a corsage on my sweater and as I wheeled my walker through the doors, I saw over one hundred familiar faces.

My strength dissolved and I fought back the tears. I was overwhelmed by the surprise and overcome with emotion. These were friends, 125 of them who loved me. I could feel their genuine caring as I passed by each and every one.

They lined up to greet me. They kissed me on my cheeks and hugged me tightly. They cried and told me things that I had done to impact their lives. They shared their memories holding my hand. One dear friend, a fiercely competitive runner told me that when she was running her longest, most difficult race she felt like quitting and then thought of what I was fighting and finished the race.

Raising funds to fight ALS

It's hard to accept such honour that people bestow on you when you're not sure what you've done to deserve it. That night I felt truly blessed, these friends raised $8,000 for ALS.

I started the drugs June 23, 2000, the day I arrived home. Twenty-four hours later I walked across the room without my walker. The gait was spastic and staggering but I felt stronger.

I also walked up the stairs unassisted clearing my foot on each step.

I was so afraid this was my mind playing games with my body. I would find out in time. We videotaped my walking and decided it would be a good thing to do every month.

Two weeks later I went in to see the doctor. He acknowledged that there was increased strength but cautioned us about being too optimistic.

I was advised by my doctor not to discuss this with anyone. How could I not be optimistic? This was a ray of hope where before there had been none.

Marc and I and the children were all optimistic. The hardest part of taking these drugs was feeling as though I was getting stronger and not being allowed to share the knowledge with other ALS patients. I felt they too should have the right to this opportunity. I understood I was a guinea pig but I knew if you asked any patient who was living with this relentless illness that they would take their chances and try the drugs.

Emotional roller coaster

One major problem was the cost of the drugs. Our benefit plan fortunately accepted the prescriptions, but for those without drug plans this would cost them at least $1,500 every month. It was an emotional roller coaster ride.

I now rejected the idea of dying but wondered every day if this was real or just a temporary plateau. Plateaus and remissions didn't happen with ALS so it was more likely that something was happening due to the medication.

I felt hopeful but confused. I wasn't in the same position anymore. I didn't feel like an ALS patient. Every day when I would wake up I would put my feet on the floor and stand.

I tested my balance and then took my steps carefully to the bathroom. The walking was still so awkward and off balance, a zigzag gait. I rejected my walker thinking that if I had to walk everywhere in the house unassisted, it would help me learn how to balance again. I started leg strengthening exercises.

There was so much that had happened in my life. And now, just because I happened to hear a story that may never have been told, I was the recipient of drugs that could possibly be my saving grace.

August 18, 2000, was the third visit to the neurologist since starting the drugs.

There was an indication of increased leg strength and it seemed less spastic.

My voice was stronger most of the time but some days I would have that feeling that there was a lump in my throat and my voice would be croaky again.

The doctor started monitoring changes and documenting for the purpose of starting a drug study with the company. Every time I went in to see him he would say "We mustn't be overly optimistic."

Feeling stronger

I wished that they had measured the strength from the days before I started of the drugs, so that we had something with which to compare it.

Marc and I were smart to have thought of video taping my gait from the start of this drug therapy.

I was going to a rehab clinic twice a week now and lifting weights. Usually the day of therapy and the day after I was worse. My muscles were tired, but on the third day I was feeling stronger. I wasn't choking on food anymore and I could swallow almost anything without difficulty.

And, my left hand was strong most of the time except at night and in the early morning.

I also noticed that I wasn't falling as much and I could move much faster. The other thing that seemed easier was turning over in bed. If this was an emotional response could my psyche sustain the improvement. Was it really measurable? I kept telling myself take one day at a time - just one. The concert kept me going.

Elizabeth's Concert of Hope

I had commitments from Michael Burgess, Andre Gagnon, Quartetto Gelato and Susan Aglukark. It was a fabulous line-up.

There were so many people who had offered to help. The committee was made up of those with professional backgrounds who knew how to move this project forward.

My vision was the driving force, but their expertise was making it happen. I didn't know how I could ever thank them for their support.

Months after I started the drugs, my strength continued to improve. On Friday, Oct 20, 2000, I had another EMG done. The Doctor is shocked at the results. It has improved from three years ago.

The doctor tells me that if the results had been the same three years ago he could not have definitively said that I had ALS back then.

He will call the drug company to arrange this drug study. I need to tell my friend Bill. It has been so hard working with him on the committee and not being able to share this secret.

I e-mailed my doctor to tell him that I couldn't lie to people anymore. They are seeing my strength and wondering why I am not declining as I had been in the winter. This needs to be made public so that all those with this disease have the same opportunity. It may only give me more time, it may not be the cure but I will take whatever it can give me.

I will continue to work at raising the profile of ALS. I am energized by my family and friends and especially by the concert and the vision I have of the evening. It will be a great success and one that will be remembered for a long while. I often wonder what will happen as with each day this story changes.

Bill has gone on the drugs for a week and has only noticed and improvement in his sleep. I still feel strong although I am not seeing any active changes at this time. Some days I feel overwhelmed by a mixture of emotions -sadness, fear and relief all at the same time. I just want stability in my life; to know one way or another what will be.

Concert a huge success

The concert was a smashing success. The night of the concert there was magic in the air. We, the committee members had been so hyped and excited for the two weeks leading up to the event.

We even felt the excitement coming from those who had bought tickets. Details for the reception had been the last priority. The value and quantity of balloon prizes were quickly growing and we had to reconsider selling balloons originally slated for $20 for $100. Some of the prizes were valued at $1,000.

Marc and the kids and I arrived a little late at the theatre. The reception started at 6:30 and by 6:45 the lobby was packed with guests.

There was a white stretch limousine sitting

outside the front doors of the venue and above the doors was the brightly lit Marquis: "Merrill Lynch presents Elizabeth's Concert of Hope" It was like a dream. Everyone was dressed up and the venue was beautifully decorated.

All the trees in the lobby were covered with tiny white sparkling white lights and there were gold and purple balloons everywhere. Shiny silver trays were filled with glasses of white wine and other trays filled with cheeses and fruits. When I walked through the doors I was surrounded by friends and family.

Nylons lend support

There were so many people I couldn't move forward to check my coat.

I manoeuvred my way through the crowd and met up with a photographer who wanted me to have my picture taken with the Nylons.

They hustled me into the theatre through the back doors and there I stood in the presence of the popular group. They were such a friendly bunch of guys. I gave them each a kiss and thanked them for their participation.

I was so honored that they had accepted at the last minute after Andre Gagnon had cancelled.

I returned to the lobby to make my way up to where the sponsors and dignitaries were gathering.

There were TV cameras following me and flashing lights.

It was strange because while the focus was on me I didn't feel at all that this was about me.

This was a celebration for the awareness and hope that could be generated from an event like this. I was engaged by the excitement.

The media were interviewing me and asking questions like: "How did all this start?" and: "Tell us why you are doing this." The story to me is so simple. I was overwhelmed by all the attention. I didn't dislike it but I felt it was misplaced. I just wanted the public and media to help raise the profile of this illness.

Now, on these drugs, I had a taste of hope. I knew how important hope was to find the energy to fight this disease. The performance was outstanding and the performers were at their best. The audience was on their feet constantly and when I walked on stage at the finale they stood for me.

An inspiring event

I know this event gave everyone in the theatre inspiration, something that we all need in our lives. It brought people together in a setting of love and caring.

It is April 2001, Bill is not improving with the drugs and I find my joints are weaker. I'm maintaining muscle strength but I'm not sure if the drugs are still working as effectively.

The same month, Canadian Living published my story. Also in April I was invited as a guest on the Viki Gabereau show.

I am still driven to continue speaking out about this illness. Recently, I spoke to 1,000 insurance brokers – we'll likely receive more financial support.

The more people that understand this terrible illness the less alone I feel. I am still strong – in fact stronger than I was two years ago. My walking hasn't improved but my clinical strength is almost normal.

The doctor does not believe that this treatment will help others. My situation is quite a paradox. It's difficult to live with a secret that might hold a clue to this disease. Because I do not feel like I'm dying now the urgency of my living has changed.

In June, 2001, the drug company approved a study of the affects of this AIDS medication on ALS. I don't know how long it will take to start the program but I feel frustrated that it has not been pushed more considering clinically it has seemed to help me.

Health problems continue

My ankle and knee and hip joints feel weaker – I don't know if it's because I'm not in a rehab program. My balance is also worse but my muscles continue to be strong. I still think there is a strong link between my motor problems and my spinal cord injury. Maybe the doctor is not looking hard enough for other factors – maybe after my next EMG – if it looks normal, he will look at other possibilities.

Later in June, 2001, we had a meeting tonight with some of the committee members to resolve some of the ongoing issues over receipting for donations.

It was a good meeting but afterward when everyone had left – my friend Bill and I sat for a bit and talked. His lower legs are virtually useless, and his left arm is weakening. He's considering renovations to the house but doesn't want to ruin the look of the house that his wife will live in after he's gone.

I felt overwhelming sadness as I was driving home but I didn't have the energy to cry and I'm not sure I have the energy to organize another concert.

I'm so afraid the second concert won't have the magic that the first one did.

I'm tired of ALS and I'm tired of being associated with the disease.

Still later in June 2001, I have had private

meetings with Minister Allan Rock and Minister Tony Clement – both have acknowledged the need for more research and support for these patients.

I was on Canada AM again and I feel it will help the cause to continue these national broadcasts – I'm just not sure I have enough energy to continue carrying the torch.

I'm tired. I hate having this secret – the AIDS cocktail! I think I'll work on another poem.

In August 2001, I find I am definitely having more difficulty with my feet and ankles.

My right ankle feels like it's sprained all the time and is always quite swollen.

It must be the way I'm walking. I feel I'm closer to needing a wheelchair that I have ever been.

In the house it's OK but to go anywhere is painfully slow with a walker and I often trip. I feel less confident about going out alone.

Friend dies from ALS

I learn that my friend Tim has died from ALS. It was such a shock.

Yet, strangely, I had been thinking about him the night he died. I think that just maybe Tim's spirit came to me.

In March 2002, we held the second Elizabeth's Concert of Hope – and it was even more wonderful than the first!

Amazing! We will do it one more time in Hamilton and then we will pass the template on to the ALS Society.

Bill is now in the monster wheelchair and is quickly losing the use of his arms.

God I don't know how I will be strong when

he is gone – he has become an important part of my life – I truly love him and all his crazy ways.

I am weakening but the disease is still progressing slowly.

I have decided to stop driving I don't feel confident behind the wheel.

I will keep writing – my style has changed somewhat, but the pleasure I get from creating poetry has not.

My two oldest children have been struggling with personal issues; identity and confidence issues.

We are trying to help them but I believe that sometimes kids have to work things out on their own. All I can do is love them.

Deceptive condition

With it being four years since my diagnosis and not having changed much in physical appearance and abilities, they see my health as relatively stable.

They don't think I'm dying. I know the disease is creeping along.

I so want them to mature quickly. I need to know that they are safe and happy, and will be able to handle their lives and all that goes along with being an independent human being. My two sisters from the west coast return to visit every six months or so. I think they feel out of the loop being so far away. They seem to want to talk about serious, deep, emotional stuff when they come back.

For me it all rolls along day to day; the only escape is sleep, when it comes.

Living with this illness has leveled my emotions but for them it returns fresh in their hearts and minds each time they come home.

My sisters and brother have been a great source of strength especially my oldest sister. She is a constant in my life, always there, always knowing what to do. Her understanding is non judgmental.

I see my parents aging quickly. Dad is ninety and Mom is eighty-four. I love them and worry about them. With their physical limitations they are becoming more and more dependant, like me.

I'm sorry I am unable to help them or Jennifer. She is the oldest and carries most of the load.

But we're all muddling along as best we can, recognizing life's blessings come in all forms. There is still plenty of laughter.

I wonder if I will still be able to laugh when I can no longer help myself.

I don't fear this stage anymore. I think I have accepted it but I know I will have to withdraw in order to cope with the pain of letting go.

A fragile shell

They say the body is just a shell but shell seekers gather shells for their beauty.

When the shell falls apart it is sometimes hard to remember how beautiful it was.

I worry about Marc. I don't think he really knows what is coming, but what would I do without him? He lives in the present, truly knowing how to take one day at a time. I think this is and will be his saving grace.

If I were in his shoes, I would be so fearful and sad to know I was losing my best friend.

I sometimes lie in bed at night and wonder what it would be like if he were dying and then no longer here.

Our twenty-seven years together now seems so short. We love each other so much and thrill in the pleasure of waking up together in the morning to share a hot coffee in front of the fire.

I relish the comfort of our small double bed. I used to think we needed a bigger one, that we were too cramped. Now I wouldn't change this bed for anything in the world.

This is our safe haven a private place for us to close the door on the day and find solace in each other.

He and our children are the greatest blessings in my life... (Elizabeth concludes her book with some Closing Thoughts, following this final selection of her poems).

The final selection of poems...

Poems
In Dreams

Elizabeth Grandbois, October 2002:
A moment of bliss...

Tickles and Whispers

Untroubled in repose,
we lie beneath lavender scented linens,
as weightless, feather pillows
cradle our tired heads.
Through the veil of night I see,
tears of affection spill and mingle
blurring the outline of you,
the rise and fall of your very being.
Our lips touch lightly,
I am suffused by the familiarity
of your warm, moist breath
again, sweet hint of your presence.
We indulge our senses
while along the length of our backs,
fingers tickle
the trials of the day away
with whispers of love.

Elizabeth Grandbois, September 2002:
Do we ever really let go of our children?

When You're Grown

I watch and wait,
I cannot say goodbye
'til you claim higher ground,
your place within in the world.
I cannot dim the light
'til I feel you strong and sure.
I watch and wait,
I will not close my eyes
'til you steer your untried ships
against the undertow of life.
And when you are grown,
I shall wait no more
for I will say goodbye
and watch.
watch over you
always,
when you are grown.

Elizabeth Grandbois, September 2002:
I like to imagine the story behind a work of art…

Obscurity in Art

*Is the art about the artist
or a world that he perceives,
is whimsy born from deep creative thought,
are the long recurrent brush strokes
losses that he grieves
or inklings of dreams that he forgot.
Does the balance in the landscape
reveal a master's kill,
coloured by the passion of his years,
will we find his soul etched
beyond the showed vale,
smudged by long forgotten tears.
Is his verity the canvas,
the heartbeat in his brush,
can a palette invite such gifted touch
does the beauty in his craft
and impression he evokes
simply evidence the sentiments he's known.*

Elizabeth Grandbois, April 2002:
A recurring nightmare…

Buried

A vague unwelcome panic
wafts through my head,
as I challenge twisted blankets.
Soundness falls away
and the nightmare settles in,
stalking fitful dreams
to haunt me once again.
Beyond advancing shadows
it creeps with furtive ease
indifferent to my pounding heart.
Tonight the shovel breaks the earth,
my body touches down
buried by the cold, dank dirt,
I strain to reach to surface,
free myself from harm,
retreating from the gentle touch
soft upon my arm.
He pulls me from this dormant hell,
echoing my name
the warm familiar presence
brings me home.
I lean into his firm embrace,
he calms my morbid fear,
and I'm coaxed once more to restful sleep.

Elizabeth Grandbois, April 2002: Sooner or later, we all near the end of our journey and face the truth…

Journey's End

Along parallel paths, we voyage through life,
arriving ultimately at the threshold.
Some stand close while others hold their distance,
some plagued by weakness,
others driven by strength,
those more willing to leap
and those reticent of stepping into darkness
beyond the chasm of doubt,
> *through the corridors of the unknown,*
> > *toward the final crescendo of light,*
> > > *the Truth of journey's end…*

Elizabeth Grandbois, January 2002:
I sometimes see myself as third person singular.

Illness

She tends
a bruised soul,
as her body
melts with merciless momentum.
Her countenance
hides the ire within.
Those few
who really see
cannot set her free.
Such pain,
poignant and prophetic,
is born from helplessness,
as she falls to the floor once more.

Mirror Image

*I stand before the looking glass,
wanting to step through
without shattering a dream,
synonymous yet separate,
you view me with questioning eyes,
I see your fear.
Mirror, mirror on the wall
who will be the first to fall?*

Farewell

*As autumn leaves fall
so fall away the secrets and lies
buried with the ashes.
Old skeletons laid to rest,
ghosts are gone.
The end of silence
brings sweet release.
Go freely,
be at peace.*

Elizabeth Grandbois, December 2001:
We would understand so much better if we could only experience what others are feeling.

Shoe Lessons

*Step out of your shoes
into mine,
I shall wear yours.
Go carefully,
the way is whorled,
the leather worn.
Dance
to my rhythm,
walk
down my road,
taste my world
and
I will sip your wine.
Fresh sentiments
leave
biases behind,
yours
and mine.*

Elizabeth Grandbois, January 2002:
Life can be so light.

Clothesline News

Clotheslines dressed haphazardly,
   denim shirts pegged at the cuffs
   billow in the wind
   resembling acrobats long forgotten,
   left to dangle
  and fade under the hot sun.
The allure of flowing lingerie,
  an enticing public display
  of slips and silk bikinis paired with camisoles,
  lace on lace,
  their gentle movements
 choreographed in the breeze.
The drollery of socks,
   knee highs and anklets, woollens and cottons,
   two left for one right,
   red, blue, black, white,
   hung by their ribs,
   heel to toe, east to west,
   they boogie wildly in the wind
  oblivious of their fabric foolery.
The unexpected birth
 of tiny, new pastel sleepers,
 minimized
 by the flailing, familiarity
 of oversized long johns,
  greying and worn at the knees,
 not quite ready for the rag bag.

*White sheets
　from a big feather bed
　flapping,
　slapping smartly at the sky,
　lined up in the queue beside old fleece towels,
　classified by colour and rank,
　their fluttering less dramatic,
　stiffening as they dry.
Clotheslines tell tales,
　　local news,
　　take care
　　as you air your laundry.*

The Lure of Sleep

*Sleep beautiful sleep,
lost in a reverie of nothing,
no consequence from nonsense,
floating from one illusion to another,
no love or pain,
loss or gain that remains
only absurdity.
Sleep never ending sleep,
beyond reality
irrational images
seduce the player,
where everything is as it should be
yet nothing is right,
save the night.
Sleep inescapable sleep,
the tonic of life.*

Elizabeth Grandbois, February 2002:
An inspiring defiance of death…

The Coral Rose

In the dead of winter's chill
a single coral rose
clings to the tip of her vine,
she refuses to surrender
to nature's ruling will
sustained by her summer bloom of pride.
Her dignity defies
the blight of northern winds,
austerity surrounds her fading blush,
the dormant buds attend her,
anchoring her stem,
awaiting to emerge from winter's hush.
And when the time is right
and the warmth of spring prevails
they will rise to veil her failing light,
their tender coral blossoms
will burn upon the bush
gracing the continuum of life.

Elizabeth Grandbois, March 2002:
Malaika is "Swahili" for angel

Malaika

*She is crystal,
clear,
except for the bubbles
caught inside her glass;
each bead a whisper of life
gently blown,
one after another
into her transparency;
sunbeams wash over her,
resplendent,
radiating
as light through a prism.
She is Malaika,
my crystalline angel.*

Elizabeth Grandbois, March 2002:
Trust is a wonderful gift, and responsibility…

Waiting for Love

I would like to walk beside you
if you'd only slow your pace,
you seem kind and today I need a friend;
I might share a little secret,
or dare to tell a tale,
in hopes that my loneliness might end.
Perhaps I'll feel your hand,
sense the warmth of your touch,
find belonging in the presence of your smile;
Indulge me in my wish
perchance to kiss your lips
or be wed to your soul for a while.
Now you blindly pass me by,
opportunity has lapsed,
I fear another kindred spirit lost,
yet, invisible as I am,
I'll return to dream again,
sustained by my willingness to trust.

Elizabeth Grandbois, March 2002:
I am very grateful to my parents, who truly made me everything I am today…

Because You Loved Me

I am who I am
because you taught me to sing
in harmony with the world.
I am who I am
because you taught me benevolence
and the beauty of butterflies.
I am who I am
because you taught me courage,
to stand firm and fair.
I am who I am
because you loved me.
For all that you are,
I know who I am
and for all that I am,
I thank you.

Elizabeth Grandbois, November 1999: Some nights are very long for me.

Night time

*Wakeful in a sleepless haze
holding fear at bay,
lying in the dark of night
willing light of day.
Planning for a peaceful rest
angels in my head,
close my eyes, fall asleep
easing awful dread.
Aware of shallow breathing
left hand like a mop,
dead weight on the lower limbs
feeling like I'm caught.
Screaming, dreaming in my head
pounding like drum,
wake me from this haunting state.
Tears upon the pillow
leave a salty stain,
wishing to escape the truth
the souvenir remains.
Drowsing in the early dawn
tranquil in my mind,
comforted by daybreak,
night time left behind...*

Elizabeth Grandbois, February 2000:
There are times when I want so badly to feel the
rhythm of movement, to move gracefully to the music,
to dance once again…

In Dreams

In dreams I am walking
nothing hinders my way,
carefree with each step I take,
movements light and gay.
Arms swing freely by my side,
companions to my feet,
my body never tires,
I move with graceful ease.
Stepping lightly as I go,
footprints in the sand,
I am lulled by the rhythm
of the cadence of the land.
I will dance to life's music,
no partner do I need,
for now I lean on no one,
I follow and I lead.
I am running,
I am leaping
and never more shall be
a prisoner of this body,
for my dreams have set me free.

Closing Thoughts:

In shaking hands with death, I have learned to embrace life. Who I was and all that I had experienced gained greater meaning once I came to terms with my own mortality.

I feel truly blessed by the love of friends and family that surround me. I will continue to be the best person, mother, wife I can be.

Initially, after suddenly being diagnosed with a terminal illness, I pulled into myself, not knowing how to respond. I had no reference points. Exhaustion and the need to confront my overwhelming fear forced me to appraise my options. How was I to deal with such frightening physical loss and what did I want to accomplish before I crossed into that unknown territory of afterlife? Would my faith be strong enough to see me through this nightmare? I realized that I did have choices and as I cautiously set my fear aside, I was more able to consider the possibilities before me.

Limited time gave urgency to my purpose.

Certainly, I knew that I wanted to leave a rich endowment of memories for my family and friends.

In doing so I needed to redefine my role as wife, mother, sister and friend, and to reinforce the spiritual connection that has always drawn us together.

Acceptance and understanding have now become conscious energies in my mothering.

Fellowship with friends and family has a new and greater significance. Attention is given to listening and sharing life experiences. I no longer feel alone or central to this difficult situation. Often, I find myself concerned for others in crisis, particularly those living with this illness. Five years after being diagnosed with

ALS, disappointment and grief lie low, somewhere beneath my heart; the cornerstone of my strength. I have accepted my illness and discovered patience and perseverance in finding purpose.

Many unexpected blessings have come from the need to trust. Adversity has strengthened my faith and given me the courage to choose transformation over defeat. I do believe my choices have affected my attitude, behavior and certainty of my relationships.

Constancy of family and friends has reassured me that in my time of greatest need I will be protected from the harshest face of illness and cocooned with caring and unconditional love.

As a child I was fortunate, life was easy and living was always secure. I thank my parents for the consistency of love and nurturing that I received. My mother showed me strength of character and my father imparted a gentle sensitivity and an appreciation of nature's wonder.

The loving connection of my siblings has always been my safety net. They are the main threads that run through my life.

My marriage has been a lesson in love, and Marc's enthusiasm has been tremendously uplifting, especially in those first two years as I battled overwhelming sadness and fear of what I was losing. With him I feel I never want to let go. We are as one.

My children bring me comfort. They are my legacy and I know I will live on in them and through their spirits. They are my world and I love them with all my heart.

In shaking hands with death, I have learned to embrace life with passion.

- *Elizabeth Grandbois*.

Editor's Note:

If you'd like to help with a donation or by volunteering your time, please contact ALS Canada at: 1-800-267-4257 or visit their website: www.als.ca.

Manor House Publishing
(905) 648-2193

www.ingramcontent.com/pod-product-compliance
Lightning Source LLC
Chambersburg PA
CBHW031254290426
44109CB00012B/583